STUNNING ANGLEPLAY™
QUILTS

◆ 6 PROJECTS ◆ 42 EXCITING BLOCKS ◆ EASY, NO-MATH PIECING

MARGARET J. MILLER

C&T PUBLISHING

Text copyright © 2008 by Margaret J. Miller

Artwork copyright © 2008 by C&T Publishing, Inc.

Publisher: Amy Marson

Editorial Director: Gailen Runge

Acquisitions Editor: Jan Grigsby

Editor: Liz Aneloski

Technical Editors: Ellen Pahl and Teresa Stroin

Copyeditor/Proofreader: Wordfirm Inc.

Cover Designer/Design Director: Christina Jarumay

Book Designer: Kerry Graham

Production Coordinator: Kirstie L. Pettersen

Illustrator: Kirstie L. Pettersen

Photography by Luke Mulks and Diane Pedersen of C&T Publishing unless otherwise noted

Published by C&T Publishing, Inc., P.O. Box 1456, Lafayette, CA 94549

Library of Congress Cataloging-in-Publication Data

Miller, Margaret J.

   Stunning AnglePlay quilts : 6 projects, 42 exciting blocks, easy, no-math piecing / Margaret J. Miller.

      p. cm.

   Summary: "A reference book of pieced blocks that include the half-rectangle triangle as a key design element. Includes instructions for 6 quilt projects"–Provided by publisher.

   Includes index.

   ISBN 978-1-57120-445-5 (paper trade : alk. paper)

   1. Quilting–Patterns. 2. Geometrical drawing. I. Title.

TT835.M5235 2008

746.46'041–dc22

                              2007032661

Printed in China

10 9 8 7 6 5 4 3 2 1

Dedication

To *Mary Hales*, my inspiration, my mentor, my friend...Thank you for all your encouragement and quiet advice over the years, and for making such a big difference in the lives of so many quiltmakers in the Pacific Northwest!

Acknowledgments

I offer my heartfelt thanks to the following people who have supported me in the writing of this book and in the making of the quilts that it showcases:

Wanda Rains, quilter extraordinaire

Sherry Loomis, who was always ready with encouragement, common sense, and lots of behind-the-scenes organization

Ruth Harris, who provided an endless supply of nurturing support and nutrition; she is also trying to teach me about rest and stopping once in a while

All my *AnglePlay workshop students*, who have greeted the AnglePlay templates and all the new possibilities they offer with such enthusiasm

Most of all, heartfelt thanks to *Liz Aneloski*, my editor, and to all the staff at C&T Publishing; it is a delight to have you on my team!

Contents

Preface

Welcome to more fun in the world of elongated triangles—the ones that make rectangles, not squares, when they are sewn together! If you have worked with the block patterns in the first book in this series, *AnglePlay™ Blocks*, you know how much fun adding this shape to the squares and half-square triangles of traditional patchwork can be!

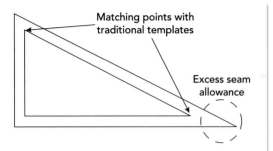

Matching points with traditional templates

Excess seam allowance

The elongated triangle shape has been difficult to piece in the past because of the excess seam allowance beyond the narrowest point. In addition, the diagonal seam does not exit the cut edge where you expect it to. Draw a square and a rectangle on a piece of paper. Draw a ¼″ seam allowance around each shape. In the square, draw a diagonal line that divides the square from corner to corner (to create half-square triangles). Note that the diagonal goes through the corners of the seamlines *and* the corners of the cutting lines.

Now draw the same diagonal line through the rectangle, being sure to line up your ruler with the corners of the *seamlines*, not the cutting line. Note that the diagonal does not exit the cutting edge in the corner! With every different size of rectangle, the diagonal exits the cut edge at a different place.

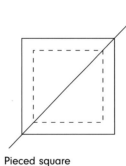

Pieced square

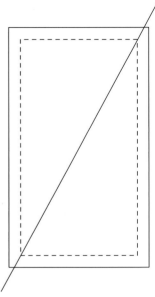

Pieced rectangle

The solution to both of these dilemmas, the excess seam allowance and nonstandard emergence of the diagonal seam through the raw edge of the patchwork shape, is AnglePlay™ templates for rotary cutting the half-rectangle shape. Each of the templates on which this book is based is trimmed at exactly the correct angle; this takes all the guesswork out of matching two fabric triangles for sewing. Moreover, the sewn results are accurate every time: The diagonal seam of the half-rectangle shape comes to the corner perfectly where units or blocks are joined together.

A few of the blocks in this book are reinterpretations of traditional blocks, but most are original blocks I developed by playing with colored paper shapes on my kitchen counter and photographing the results. So many blocks emerged (I stopped myself from generating more of them at block number 233!) that I eventually used the computer program EQ5 to organize them and to develop even more designs.

Welcome to the wide world of AnglePlay!

CHAPTER 1

Introduction

HOW TO USE THIS BOOK

The books in the AnglePlay series will soon become mainstays in your library of quiltmaking basics because they are reference books of pieced blocks that include the elongated triangle as a key design element. The list of your favorite patchwork block patterns will expand significantly with the addition of this hitherto unexplored shape, destined to be the next classic shape in American patchwork design.

First peruse the Gallery of Blocks, beginning on page 12, to see which blocks strike your fancy. Next, look at Block Patterns, beginning on page 16, where the blocks are portrayed as shaded diagrams, and see which blocks draw your attention; they may or may not match the ones you liked in the colored illustrations! This chapter presents the information you need to make a block, identifying the specific templates needed and other shapes to cut to make a 12″ finished block.

If you own a set of AnglePlay templates, you are ready to start cutting out fabric. If not, you can make your own set out of template plastic, using the drawings in Appendix A (beginning on page 57).

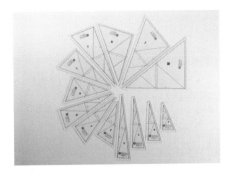

If you would like to follow a pattern for your first AnglePlay quilt, see Making AnglePlay Quilts (beginning on page 28) for six quilt design possibilities. There you will see plans for quilts of different sizes, some with blocks set straight and others with blocks on point.

Some quilts contain pairs of blocks such that when you place them side by side, you camouflage where one block stops and its neighbor begins. Play with tessellations, directional block patterns, and sampler quilts with a refreshing new look. This chapter will also help you play with different sizes of blocks and block elements, and with blocks offset from each other. The chapter also shows you how to look at blocks differently. You will play with Four-Patch blocks in a new way, by rotating their quadrants. Also, you will see how to create multiple versions of a block by dropping design lines one at a time.

You can see my book *Smashing Sets: Exciting Ways to Arrange Quilt Blocks* for more plans for quilts to house your AnglePlay blocks. Make your own choices of specific AnglePlay or other quilt blocks to plug into these plans.

SUPPLIES

Use good-quality, high-thread-count fabrics. You will be cutting across the grain of the fabric at many bias angles, and a higher-thread-count fabric will not distort and stretch as much as one with a lower thread count. Try to use a complete range of values (light to medium to dark). You will find that prints blend more

easily than solids. Many quilts in this book feature striped fabrics or variegated fabrics (which move from light to dark, or from one scale of print to another across the fabric).

Use fine, thin straight pins rather than standard pins. Thinner pins distort the bias edge less and are easier to use. I like thin pins with a large round head for easy retrieval.

The templates will remain accessible on your worktable if they are standing upright in a slotted stand. Template racks are available from your local quilt shop or from the source listed in Resources (page 62).

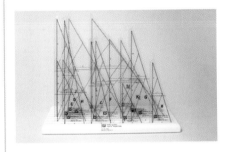

Use a sharp blade in your rotary cutter (to save wear and tear on your wrists, hands, and fingers). Do not try to cut through more than six layers of fabric. Since you must cut four sides of the template to create this shape, use a small cutting mat that you can rotate. That way you can cut two sides of the template and then rotate the cutting mat, and you will not have to disturb the positioning of the template on the fabric to make the last two cuts.

If you choose to use the drawings in Appendix A to create your own templates, be sure to trace and cut these *very* carefully and use the sturdiest (thickest) transparent template plastic your quilt shop has to offer.

Clear template plastic is easier to use for this process than plastic with a grid printed on it. Of course, in order to create the block in fabric, you will have the added step of tracing around the plastic template before cutting it out. You can still cut several layers of fabric at a time, but be sure that the shape is traced carefully and accurately.

CUTTING GUIDE

Working with directional triangles may seem a little awkward at first, but soon you will be cutting long triangles like the wind! You are guaranteed to have some unused triangles left over after every project; these can be likened to sourdough starter...ready to start the next quilt!

Cutting Traditional Shapes

AnglePlay elongated triangles are used in conjunction with squares, rectangles, half-square triangles, and quarter-square triangles. These additional shapes can be rotary cut, according to the following guidelines.

Squares and Rectangles: Cut fabric ½" larger than the desired finished measurement.

Half-Square Triangles: Cut a square of fabric ⅞" larger than the desired finished measurement, then cut in half from corner to corner.

Quarter-Square Triangles: Cut a square 1¼" larger than the desired finished measurement. Then, cut it in half from corner to corner both ways.

Cutting Full-Size AnglePlay Shapes

On each AnglePlay template, there are two sizes of triangles; one is full size and the other is half size.

Pay attention to how you position the template on the fabric, so that the straight grain runs along the edges of the pieced rectangle. The diagonal seam should be the only one that is on the bias, unless you are using a directional print or stripe that would require you to position the template otherwise.

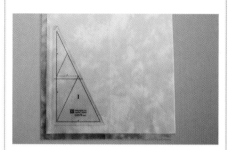

Note that there are "right-facing" triangles, abbreviated as **RFT**, and "left-facing" triangles, abbreviated as **LFT**. The block or design you choose will dictate which one you cut. In most cases, cut with your fabrics right side up and flip the template over as necessary.

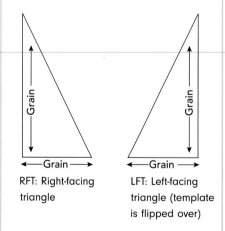

RFT: Right-facing triangle

LFT: Left-facing triangle (template is flipped over)

If you are making a directional block such as a Pinwheel, cutting the fabric just as it comes from the bolt (one layer right side up, the other wrong side up) will result in pinwheels that spin in opposite directions. This could make for a more interesting quilt than one in which all the blocks look exactly the same.

To cut a single shape from a large piece of fabric, position the template near the corner of the fabric. Make the first two cuts so you can move the bulk of the fabric away from the cutting area; then rotate the small cutting mat to cut the other two sides of the triangle.

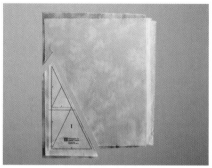

Shortcuts to Cutting Multiple Triangles

If your pattern calls for multiple triangles of the same kind (either RFT or LFT), cut a strip of fabric that is 1½" wider than the long dimension of your template. For example, template I measures 4" × 8" finished (the finished dimensions are printed on the templates); cut a strip 9½" wide across the width of your fabric. Cut along the fold and layer both fabric strips right sides up. Cut the template shape once, then rotate it to cut the next one, and so on.

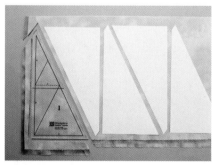

Paper mock-ups show how template can be rotated to cut multiple triangles along strip of fabric.

You may work with more than two layers of fabric if your pattern calls for a large number of the same template; just be sure that all layers are right side up and that you have the template positioned properly to get the triangle you want.

If you need only four of the same triangle, cut two rectangles that are 1½" wider and longer than the finished size of the triangle. For example, if you need four of template E, RFT, cut the rectangles 4½" × 7½" since E finishes at 3" × 6". Place both rectangles right side up, place the template about ¼" from the raw edges, and cut diagonally. Then, stack all four fabric triangles together right sides up, position the template, and cut four E triangles at once.

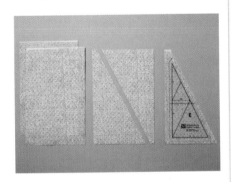

Cutting Half-Size AnglePlay Shapes

1. To cut a half-size shape, square up a piece of fabric using the straight-grain lower corner (right angle) of the template.

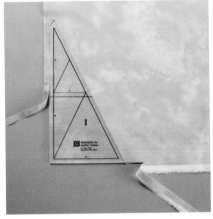

2. Slide the template down so that one cut edge of the fabric aligns with the solid baseline of the smaller triangle. Align the straight-grain side of the template with the other cut edge of the fabric.

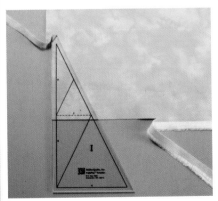

Cut along the diagonal edge and along the tip of the triangle.

Making Pieced Triangles

Each template has a diagonal line that cuts the triangle in half, from the straight-grain corner to the midpoint of the opposite edge. I call this the half-diagonal line. With this line you can create a pieced triangle that will greatly expand the number and type of blocks you can make. You can get a much more complex-looking design from simple shapes, often creating a three-dimensional look on the two-dimensional surface.

To create a pieced triangle, you will rough cut the half-triangle pieces first and sew them together. Then you will position your template to cut the final pieced triangle, aligning the half-diagonal line on the template with your sewn seam. In the instructions that follow, the long narrow side triangle is called A, and the other base triangle is called B. The seam that joins them is called the half diagonal.

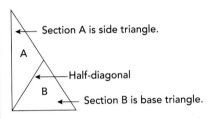

Cutting Section A: Side Triangle

1. Place the template on the fabric so that the long straight-grain edge of side triangle is "in your lap" (toward you) and at least ½" from the fabric edge. Beginning about ⅔ of the way up from the tip of the triangle, cut along the diagonal (bias edge), off the edge of the fabric.

2. Fold back the cut edge of fabric beyond the template and flip the template over so that the long edge is still on the straight grain. Slide the template back toward the first cut edge so *both* the long edge of the triangle *and* the half-diagonal line on the template are about ½" away from their respective fabric edges. Cut along the diagonal (bias edge) and off the edge of the fabric.

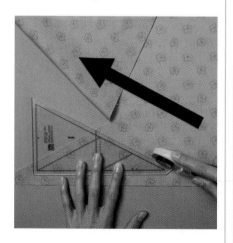

Cutting Section B: Base Triangle

1. Place the template on the fabric so that the straight-grain edge of the side triangle is "in your lap" (toward you) and the straight-grain edge of the base triangle is at least ½" from the fabric edge. Proceed as you did with side triangle A; beginning about ⅔ of the way from the lower right triangle point, cut along the diagonal (bias edge), off the edge of the fabric.

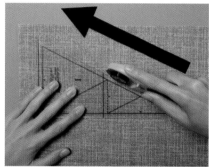

2. Rotate the cutting mat so that the straight-grain edge of the base triangle is "in your lap." Fold back the cut edge of the fabric beyond the template, and flip the template over so that the base (short straight edge) of the template is still on the straight grain. Slide the template back toward your first cut edge so *both* the base edge of the triangle *and* the half-diagonal line on the template are about ½" away from their respective fabric edges. Cut along the second bias edge of the base triangle and off the edge of the fabric.

Note that Sections A and B can make either a right-facing or a left-facing triangle. You can make the first cut with the template right side or reverse side up; simply flip it over to make the second cut. Also note that A and B are only rough cut; they are considerably larger than what you need.

Joining Sections A and B

1. Align the A and B pieces along the half-diagonal seam. Sew them together using a ¼" seam. Since the rough edges will soon be trimmed, you don't have to align pieces A and B carefully at this point. Press the seam open.

2. Reposition the template on the joined fabrics, aligning the half-diagonal line on the template with the sewn seam. Rotary cut around the template.

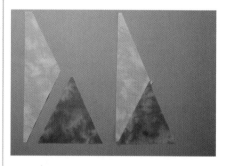

PIECING TIPS

Before sewing any triangles together, take a template to the sewing machine and place it under the presser foot. Lower the needle so it touches the seamline on the template. Notice where the edge of the template aligns on your machine's throat plate. This is where the raw edges of the triangles should align as you sew the triangles together. You can add a line of ¼" masking tape as a guide if you want. *This may or may not be what you currently use as your ¼" seam guide.*

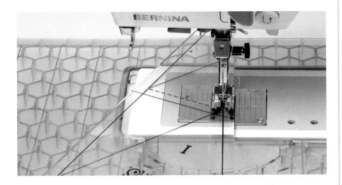

Since you will begin to sew the seam at the point of the triangles, be sure to hold both threads (top and bobbin) taut behind the presser foot as you take the first stitches. This will keep the beginning of the seam from disappearing down through your machine's throat plate, making an annoying mess.

Piecing Order

Start with the shortest seams and work toward the longer ones. Sew all the diagonal seams first; then join the resulting squares and rectangles into rows or into larger pieced units.

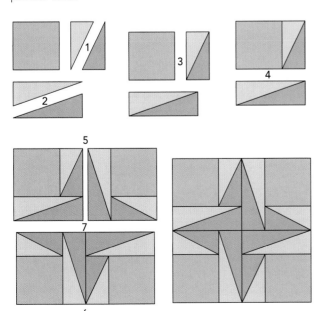

Piecing Tray

If you have several of the same block to make for a given quilt, a piecing tray is an invaluable tool. This is simply a large piece of graph paper with the full-size block units drawn on it. You can place it on a tray or an extra cutting mat for stability.

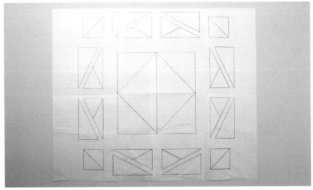

Draw block units on large piece of graph paper; leave space between units to accommodate fabric shapes with seam allowances.

Fabric shapes on top of paper piecing tray; use cutting mat under fabric and paper so piecing tray can be transported from design wall to sewing table. As piecing proceeds, block will appear smaller and smaller.

Stack the pieces in place on a tray and use chain-piecing methods to speed the sewing process.

Partial-Seam Construction

Several of the blocks in this book require partial-seam construction. This technique makes it easy to sew blocks that look complex. Blocks that require this approach have a square unit in the center and are framed by rectangular or other pieced units. The center square can be a single patch or a pieced unit. Quilts in which blocks have been offset also require this technique.

Here are two examples of blocks that require partial seams.

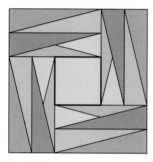
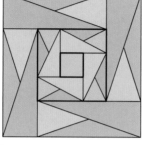

Cornfield   Pixie Dust (two partial seams)

1. With right sides together, align the center square with the adjacent rectangular unit. Sew the square about halfway across, or stop stitching at least 1″ from the edge, leaving the remainder of the piece free. Press.

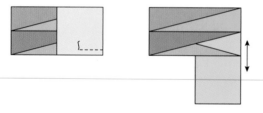

2. Align the next unit, right sides together, and stitch the second seam. Work your way around the block, adding each unit in order. Then complete the partial seam between the final unit and the first unit. Press.

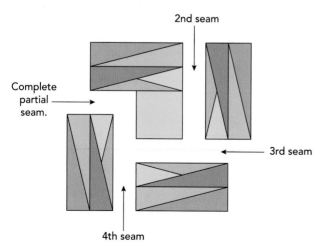

2nd seam

Complete partial seam.

3rd seam

4th seam

Piecing Accuracy

The templates are designed so that you will be able to line up two triangles quickly and easily, using the angle you cut at the narrow point. This works like a dream! Also, the trimmed narrow point produces less bulk where the pieced units come together at the corners.

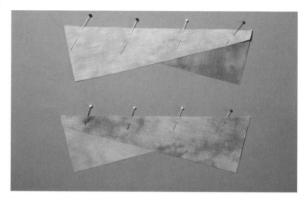

Align triangles and pin.

Careful pinning helps yield precise piecing. Use thin straight pins (silk pins work well) for the least distortion of the bias edge. Press all seams open. This distributes the bulk of the seam allowances as evenly as possible, regardless of the angle of the seams coming into the joining of four blocks.

When you begin to sew together pieces for your quilt, check after sewing the first seam to be sure that the diagonal seam will meet the corner properly and that your pieced rectangles are the correct size. To do this, draw the finished size of the rectangle you are making on a piece of graph paper and add the ¼″ seam allowance all around. Draw the diagonal of the *finished size* rectangle from corner to corner, and extend it out beyond the outer rectangle.

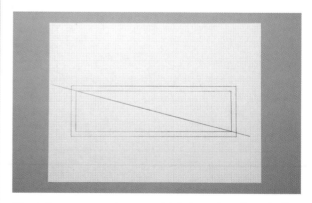

Place the sewn and pressed fabric rectangle onto the graph paper drawing.

Right

Wrong

Is the sewn rectangle the same size as the drawing? Does the sewn seam exit the rectangle at the same place it does on the paper? If not, check the seam allowance you used with a template to make sure that you are *sewing* the same seam allowance you *cut* with the AnglePlay templates.

When joining rows of units with two seams to match, roll back the top layer to align the two seams; then unroll so the raw edges are even and pin on both sides of the seam.

Aligning seams to be matched

When joining pieces together, note that there is no corner to match up on rectangles that are made of

AnglePlay triangles. Therefore, to match corners accurately, match the two adjacent raw edges, not the corner.

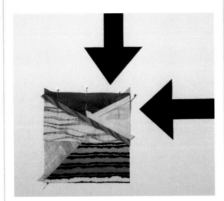

◆ Hint

When joining units in which more than two seams meet at one point, place a pin through the seam at the finished corner point of first one unit, then through the corresponding point on its mate, to ensure precise piecing.

This technique is also useful when joining rows or larger units of pieced rectangles. Place the units to be joined right sides together, and place a pin through the precise points that you want to meet at the seam. Leave that pin perpendicular to the fabric.

Pin normally on each side of the perpendicular pin. Pin the rest of the seam in preparation for sewing.

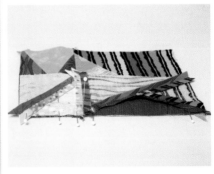

Leave the perpendicular pin in place until you can't sew any further without removing it.

With this method, your seamlines will meet precisely and you will have nice sharp points.

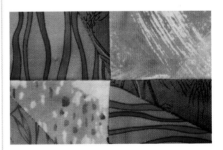

Working with the half-rectangle shape and with the AnglePlay templates will help you develop your precision and craftsmanship in sewing patchwork blocks and quilts. You will improve your piecing skills, almost in spite of yourself!

This chapter provides an overview of the blocks, in color and fabric. I tried to use as many different colors as I could, and I included the complete spectrum of light to dark values. Play with your own favorite colors and try reversing the positions of lights and darks to see yet more versions of the same designs.

Under the illustrations of each block are listed the block name and the page where the shaded block diagram and piecing diagram appear. The shaded version of the block includes light, medium, and dark values. In many cases, the value placements in the shaded illustrations are different from those in the colored photos in this chapter. This is intentional, to show you how different these blocks can look.

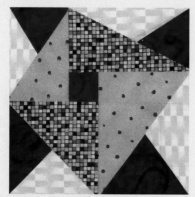

Peep Hole (page 19)

Swallowtail (page 18)

Gypsy Rose (page 20)

Cheerleader (page 17)

Formal Dance (page 17)

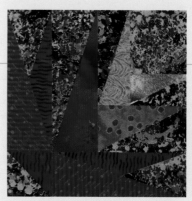

Succulent (page 19)

Marigold (page 18)

Half & Half (page 19)

Prop Plane (page 17)

Reserve Energy (page 18)

Prickly Pear (page 20)

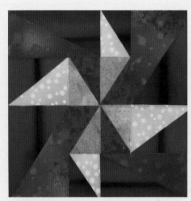

Sparkler (page 21)

Stars Over Seattle (page 17)

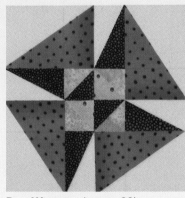

Bun Warmer (page 20)

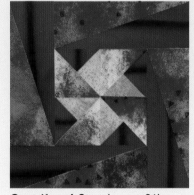

Centrifugal Star (page 21)

No Bed of Roses (page 18)

Courtyard (page 20)

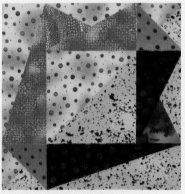

Masquerade (page 21)

Baby Birds (page 22)

Harlequin (page 21)

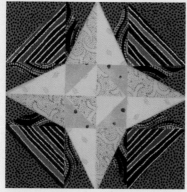

Star Search (page 23)

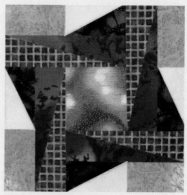

Braided Bounds (page 22)

Double Star (page 23)

Sparkle Plenty (page 24)

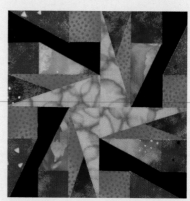

Park Place (page 22)

Neatly Folded (page 24)

Nestled In (page 24)

Scout's Star (page 22)

Around the World (page 26)

Swallow's Turning (page 24)

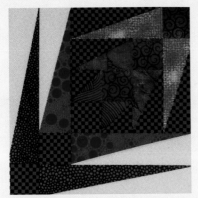
Topsy-Turvy (page 27)

Clamshell (page 27)

Okanogan (page 25)

Who's Starry Now? (page 25)

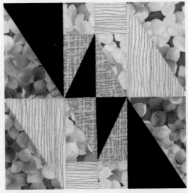
Argyle Socks (page 26)

Pageboy (page 25)

Cornfield (page 23)

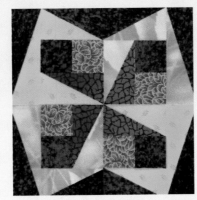
Clockwork (page 26)

Boxed In (page 26)

Show Lights (page 23)

Moving Boxes (page 27)

Spinning Wheel (page 25)

CHAPTER 3

Block Patterns

This chapter includes cutting charts and all the information needed to make the AnglePlay blocks presented in Chapter 2.

HOW TO USE THE DIAGRAMS AND CHARTS

Each block is presented first in a colored, shaded diagram with the dimensions of the major units along the edges of the block. All the blocks will finish at 12″ square.

The second illustration is a piecing diagram with a number for each patch. The chart lists the patch numbers and how many to cut of each. The letters in the chart refer to the letters on the template patterns in Appendix A (pages 57–61), which correspond to the letters on the AnglePlay templates. If the template letter has the number 1 after it, cut the half-size triangle in the upper portion of the template.

I have kept the cutting charts as simple as possible to give you freedom to vary the values and value placements. This gives you many different possible looks for any block. When a cutting chart indicates that you are to cut "3 ea: B" for Patch "3, 4," this means that you need to cut three of Template B for each Patch 3 and 4, for a total of 6 patches. You will need to determine how many B patches of each value or color to cut. Choose fabric colors and values carefully to achieve the necessary contrast.

The icons in the charts represent the shapes you will be cutting. When the icons are divided along the half-diagonal, you need to rough cut the shapes first and then piece them. Refer to Making Pieced Triangles (pages 7–8) for details.

◆ Reducing Block Size

If a block is very simple, with few pieces, such as Baby Birds (page 22), it can be created as a 6″ block by using the smaller (half-size) triangles on the listed templates. For a smaller version of more complex blocks, such as Sparkle Plenty (page 24), I recommend foundation piecing. To do this, draft the 6″ block on paper, divide it into units as shown in the piecing diagram, and copy onto your preferred foundation.

Symbols for cutting charts

Square

Half-square triangle

Quarter-square triangle

Rectangle

Half-rectangle triangle

Pieced half-rectangle triangle

AnglePlay template

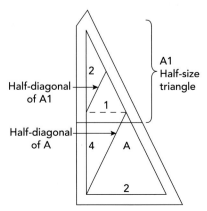

Half-diagonal of A1

A1 Half-size triangle

Half-diagonal of A

Numbers indicate finished size in inches.

THE BLOCKS

 ## *Prop Plane*

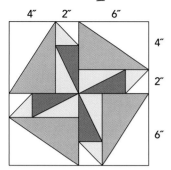

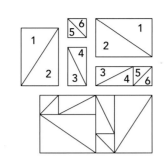

Patch	Cut		Subcut	
1, 2	4 ea: H			
3, 4	4 ea: A			
5, 6	2 ea: 2⅞"		4 ea:	

Templates: A, H; Color photo on page 13

 ## *Stars Over Seattle*

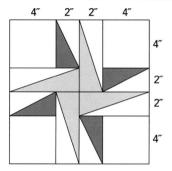

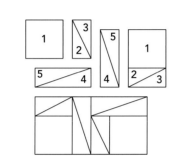

Patch	Cut	
1	4: 4½"	
2, 3	4 ea: A	
4, 5	4 ea: B	

Templates: A, B; Color photo on page 13

 ## *Cheerleader*

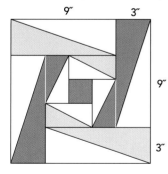

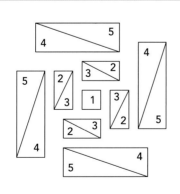

Patch	Cut	
1	1: 2½"	
2, 3	4 ea: A	
4, 5	4 ea: G	

Templates: A, G; Color photo on page 12

Note: Sew this block together with a partial seam. See Partial-Seam Construction on page 10.

 ## *Formal Dance*

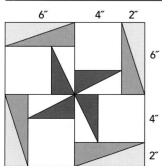

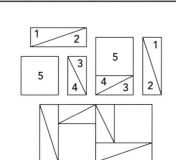

Patch	Cut	
1, 2	4 ea: B	
3, 4	4 ea: A	
5	4: 4½"	

Templates: A, B; Color photo on page 12

No Bed of Roses

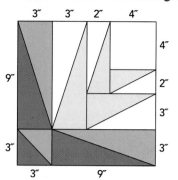

Patch	Cut		Subcut	
1	1: 4½″ ☐			
2, 3	1 ea: A ◺			
4, 5	1 ea: B ◺			
6, 7	1 ea: E ◺			
8, 9	2 ea: G ◺			
10, 11	1 ea: G ◺			
12, 13	1 ea: 3⅞″ ☐		1 ea: ◺	

Templates: A, B, E, G; Color photo on page 13

 # *Swallowtail*

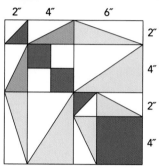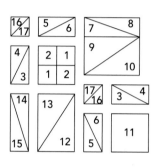

Patch	Cut		Subcut	
1, 2	2 ea: 2½″ ☐			
3, 4	2 ea: A ◺			
5, 6	2 ea: A ◺			
7, 8	1 ea: B ◺			
9, 10	1 ea: H ◺			
11	1: 4½″ ☐			
12, 13	1 ea: H ◺			
14, 15	1 ea: B ◺			
16, 17	1 ea: 2⅞″ ☐		2 ea: ◺	

Templates: A, B, H; Color photo on page 12

 # *Marigold*

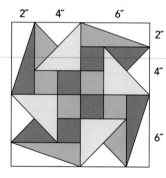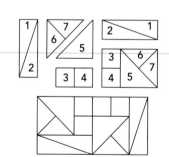

Patch	Cut		Subcut	
1, 2	4 ea: B ◺			
3, 4	4 ea: 2½″ ☐			
5	2: 4⅞″ ☐		4: ◺	
6, 7	1 ea: 5¼″ ☐		4 ea: ◺	

Template: B; Color photo on page 13

 # *Reserve Energy*

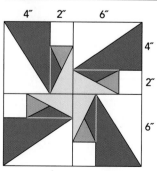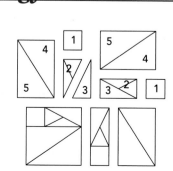

Patch	Cut	
1	4: 2½″ ☐	
2	4: A ◺	
3	4: A ◺	
4, 5	4 ea: H ◺	

Templates: A, H; Color photo on page 13

Succulent

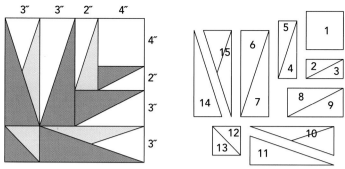

Templates: A, B, E, G; Color photo on page 12

Patch	Cut	Subcut
1	1: 4½" □	
2, 3	1 ea: A ◺	
4, 5	1 ea: B ◺	
6, 7	1 ea: G ◺	
8, 9	1 ea: E ◺	
10	1: G ◺	
11	1: G ◺	
12, 13	1 ea: 3⅞" □	1 ea: ◺
14	1: G ◺	
15	1: G ◺	

Peep Hole

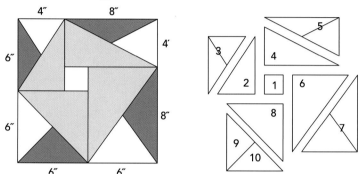

Templates: H, I, K; Color photo on page 12

Note: Sew this block together with a partial seam.
See Partial-Seam Construction on page 10.

Patch	Cut	Subcut
1	1: 2½" □	
2	1: H ◺	
3	1: H ◺	
4	1: I ◺	
5	1: I ◺	
6	1: K ◺	
7	1: K ◺	
8	1: 6⅞" □	1: ◺
9, 10	1 ea: 7¼" □	1 ea: ▽

Half & Half

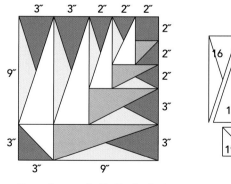

Templates: A, B, E, G; Color photo on page 13

Patch	Cut	Subcut
1	1: 2½" □	
2, 3	1 ea: 2⅞" □	1 ea: ◺
4	1: A ▷	
5	1: A ◺	
6	1: A ◹	
7	1: A ◺	
8	1: B ▷	
9	1: B ◺	
10	1: E ◿	
11	1: E ◺	
12, 16	1 ea: G ◺	
13, 17	1 ea: G ◺	
14	1: G ◿	
15	1: G ◺	
18, 19	1 ea: 3⅞" □	1 ea: ◺

Prickly Pear

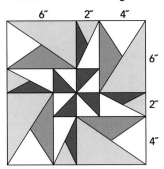

Patch	Cut		Subcut	
1	4: H	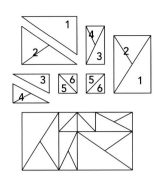		
2	4: H			
3	4: A			
4	4: A			
5, 6	2 ea: 2⅞"		4 ea:	

Templates: A, H; Color photo on page 13

Bun Warmer

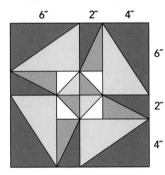

Patch	Cut		Subcut	
1, 2	4 ea: H			
3, 4	2 ea: 2⅞"		4 ea:	
5, 6	4 ea: A			

Templates: A, H; Color photo on page 13

Courtyard

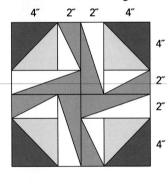

Patch	Cut		Subcut	
1, 2	2 ea: 4⅞"		4 ea:	
3, 4	4 ea: A			
5, 6	4 ea: B			

Templates: A, B; Color photo on page 13

Gypsy Rose

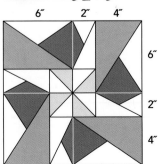

Patch	Cut		Subcut	
1	4: H			
2	4: H			
3	4: A			
4	4: A			
5, 6	2 ea: 2⅞"		4 ea:	

Templates: A, H; Color photo on page 12

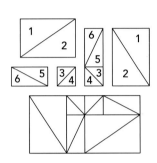
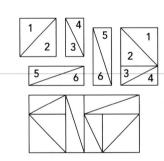
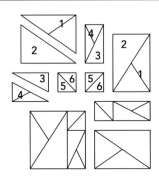

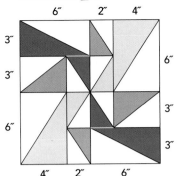

Sparkler

 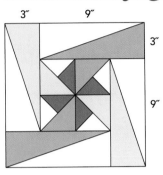 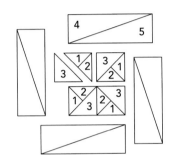

Patch	Cut	
1, 2	2 ea: E	△
3, 4, 7, 8	2 ea: H1	◿
5, 6	2 ea: K1	◺
9, 10	2 ea: H1	◺
11, 12	2 ea: H	◹

Templates: E, H, H1, K1; Color photo on page 13

 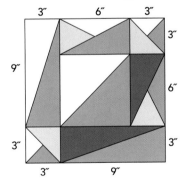 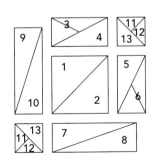

Centrifugal Star

Patch	Cut		Subcut	
1, 2	1 ea: $4\frac{1}{4}''$	☐	4 ea:	▽
3	2: $3\frac{7}{8}''$	☐	4:	◺
4, 5	4 ea: G	◺		

Template: G; Color photo on page 13

Note: Sew this block together with a partial seam. See Partial-Seam Construction on pages 10.

 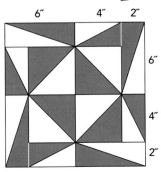 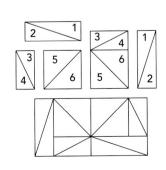

Masquerade

Patch	Cut		Subcut	
1, 2	1 ea: $6\frac{7}{8}''$	☐	1 ea:	◺
3	1: E	◿		
4	1: E	◹		
5	1: E	◹		
6	1: E	◹		
7, 8	1 ea: G	◺		
9, 10	1 ea: G	◿		
11, 12	1 ea: $4\frac{1}{4}''$	☐	2 ea:	▽
13	1: $3\frac{7}{8}''$	☐	2:	◺

Templates: E, G; Color photo on page 13

Harlequin

Patch	Cut		Subcut	
1, 2	4 ea: B	◹		
3, 4	4 ea: A	◿		
5, 6	2 ea: $4\frac{7}{8}''$	☐	4 ea:	◺

Templates: A, B; Color photo on page 14

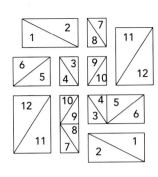

Baby Birds

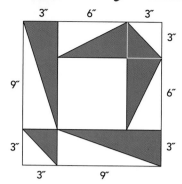

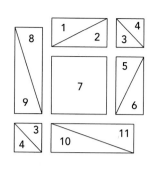

Patch	Cut		Subcut
1, 2	1 ea: E	◹	
3, 4	1 ea: 3⅞″ ▢		2 ea: ◺
5, 6	1 ea: E	◺	
7	1: 6½″ ▢		
8, 9	1 ea: G	◺	
10, 11	1 ea: G	◺	

Templates: E, G; Color photo on page 14

Park Place

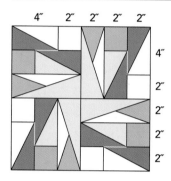

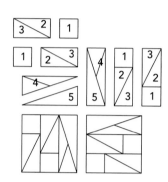

Patch	Cut	
1	8: 2½″ ▢	
2, 3	8 ea: A	◹
4	4: B	◺
5	4: B	◺

Templates: A, B; Color photo on page 14

Scout's Star

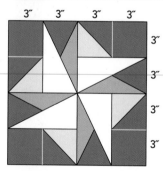

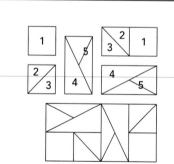

Patch	Cut		Subcut
1	4: 3½″ ▢		
2, 3	2 ea: 3⅞″ ▢		4 ea: ◺
4	4: E	◹	
5	4: E	◺	

Template: E; Color photo on page 14

Braided Bounds

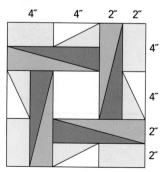

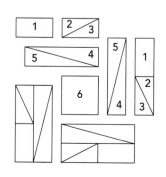

Patch	Cut	
1	4: 2½″ × 4½″ ▭	
2, 3	4 ea: A	◹
4, 5	4 ea: C	◺
6	1: 4½″ ▢	

Templates: A, C; Color photo on page 14

Note: Sew this block together with a partial seam. See Partial-Seam Construction on page 10.

Double Star

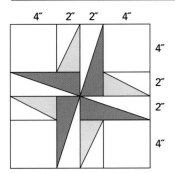

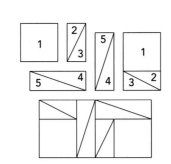

Patch	Cut	
1	4: 4½"	☐
2, 3	4 ea: A	◁
4, 5	4 ea: B	◁

Templates: A, B; Color photo on page 14

 ## *Cornfield*

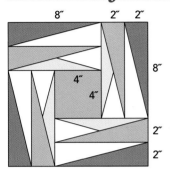

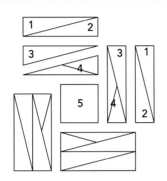

Patch	Cut	
1, 2, 3	4 ea: C	◁
4	4: C	◁
5	1: 4½"	☐

Template: C; Color photo on page 15

Note: Sew this block together with a partial seam. See Partial-Seam Construction on page 10.

 ## *Show Lights*

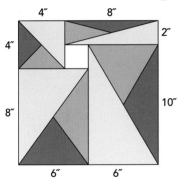

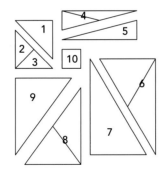

Patch	Cut		Subcut	
1	1: 4⅞"	☐	1:	◁
2, 3	1 ea: 5¼"	☐	1 ea:	▽
4	1: C	◁		
5	1: C	◁		
6	1: L	◁		
7	1: L	◁		
8	1: K	◁		
9	1: K	◁		
10	1: 2½"	☐		

Templates: C, K, L; Color photo on page 15

Note: Sew this block together with a partial seam. See Partial-Seam Construction on page 10.

 ## *Star Search*

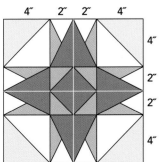

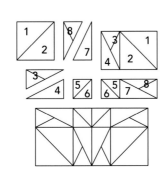

Patch	Cut		Subcut	
1, 2	2 ea: 4⅞"	☐	4 ea:	◁
3	4: A	◁		
4	4: A	◁		
5, 6	2 ea: 2⅞"	☐	4 ea:	◁
7	4: A	◁		
8	4: A	◁		

Template: A; Color photo on page 14

Sparkle Plenty

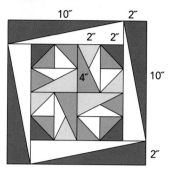

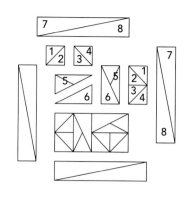

Patch	Cut		Subcut	
1, 2, 3, 4	2 ea: 2⅞″		4 ea:	
5	4: A			
6	4: A			
7, 8	4 ea: D			

Templates: A, D; Color photo on page 14

Note: Sew the outer portion of this block together with a partial seam. See Partial-Seam Construction on page 10.

Nestled In

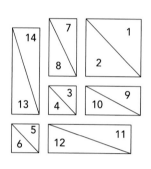

Patch	Cut		Subcut	
1, 2	1 ea: 6⅞″		1 ea:	
3, 4, 5, 6	1 ea: 3⅞″		1 ea:	
7, 8	1 ea: E			
9, 10	1 ea: E			
11, 12	1 ea: G			
13, 14	1 ea: G			

Templates: E, G; Color photo on page 14

Swallow's Turning

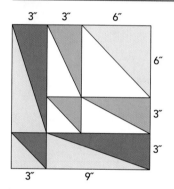

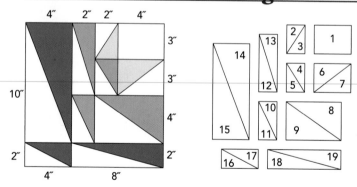

Patch	Cut	
1	1: 3½″ × 4½″	
2, 3	1 ea: H1	
4, 5	1 ea: H1	
6, 7	1 ea: K1	
8, 9	1 ea: H	
10, 11	1 ea: A	
12, 13	1 ea: B	
14, 15	1 ea: J	
16, 17	1 ea: A	
18, 19	1 ea: C	

Templates: A, B, C, H, H1, J, K1; Color photo on page 14

Neatly Folded

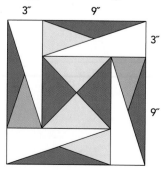

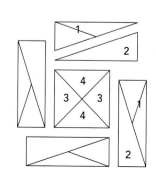

Patch	Cut		Subcut	
1	4: G			
2	4: G			
3, 4	1 ea: 7¼″		2 ea:	

Template: G; Color photo on page 14

Note: Sew this block together with a partial seam. See Partial-Seam Construction on page 10.

Okanogan

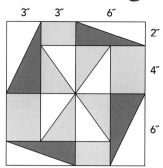

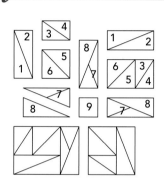

Patch	Cut	
1, 2	2 ea: E	◿
3	2: 2½″ × 3½″	▭
4, 5	2 ea: K1	◹
6, 7	2 ea: K1	◺
8, 9	2 ea: B	◿
10	2: 3½″ × 4½″	▭

Templates: B, E, K1; Color photo on page 15

Who's Starry Now?

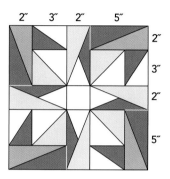

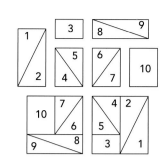

Patch	Cut		Subcut	
1, 2	4 ea: J1	◿		
3, 4	4 ea: H1	◺		
5, 6	2 ea: 3⅞″	▭	4 ea:	◺
7	4: J1	◺		
8	4: J1	◺		
9	1: 2½″	▭		

Templates: H1, J1; Color photo on page 15

Spinning Wheel

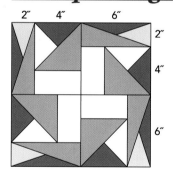

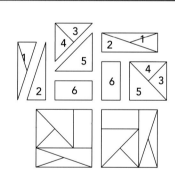

Patch	Cut		Subcut	
1	4: B	◺		
2	4: B	◺		
3, 4	1 ea: 5¼″	▭	4 ea:	▽
5	2: 4⅞″	▭	4:	◺
6	4: 2½″ × 4½″	▭		

Template: B; Color photo on page 15

Pageboy

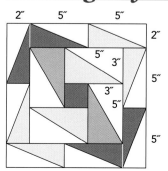

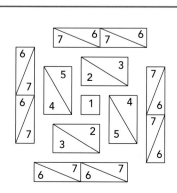

Patch	Cut	
1	1: 2½″	▭
2, 3	2 ea: L1	◺
4, 5	2 ea: L1	◹
6, 7	8 ea: J1	◺

Templates: J1, L1; Color photo on page 15

Note: Sew this block together with a partial seam. See Partial-Seam Construction on page 10.

Around the World

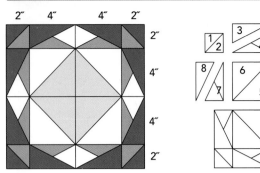

Patch	Cut		Subcut	
1, 2	2 ea: 2⅞″	☐	4 ea:	◺
3	4: A	◿		
4	4: A	◺		
5, 6	2 ea: 4⅞″	☐	4 ea:	◺
7	4: A	▷		
8	4: A	▷		

Template: A; Color photo on page 14

 ## *Clockwork*

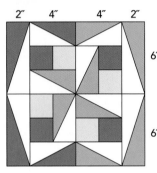
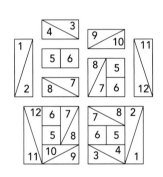

Patch	Cut	
1, 2	2 ea: B	◿
3, 4,	2 ea: A	▷
5, 6	4 ea: 2½″	☐
7, 8	4 ea: A	▷
9, 10	2 ea: A	◿
11, 12	2 ea: B	◹

Templates: A, B; Color photo on page 15

 ## *Argyle Socks*

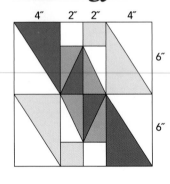
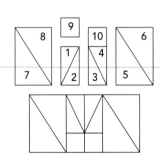

Patch	Cut	
1, 2	2 ea: A	▷
3, 4	2 ea: A	◿
5, 6, 7, 8	2 ea: H	◺
9, 10	2 ea: 2½″	☐

Templates: A, H; Color photo on page 15

 ## *Boxed In*

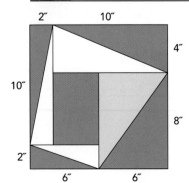
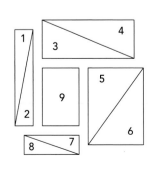

Patch	Cut	
1, 2	1 ea: D	◺
3, 4	1 ea: J	◺
5, 6	1 ea: K	◹
7, 8	1 ea: B	▷
9	1: 4½″ × 6½″	▭

Templates: B, D, J, K; Color photo on page 15

Note: Sew this block together with a partial seam. See Partial-Seam Construction on page 10.

Topsy-Turvy

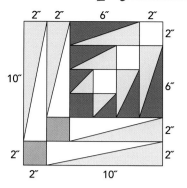

Templates: A, B, C, D; Color photo on page 15

Patch	Cut	Subcut
1, 2	1 ea: 2⅞″ □	2 ea: ◁
3	6: 2½″ □	
4, 5	1 ea: A ◿	
6, 7	1 ea: A ▷	
8, 9	1 ea: B ◿	
10, 11	1 ea: B ▷	
12, 13	1 ea: C ▷	
14, 15	1 ea: C ◿	
16, 17	1 ea: D ▷	
18, 19	1 ea: D ◿	

Clamshell

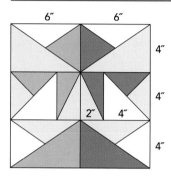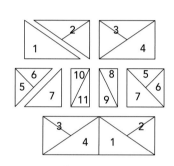

Patch	Cut	Subcut
1	2: H ◺	
2	2: H ◹	
3	2: H ◿	
4	2: H ◿	
5, 6	1 ea: 5¼″ □	2 ea: ▽
7	1: 4⅞″ □	2: ◺
8, 9	1 ea: A ◿	
10, 11	1 ea: A ▷	

Templates: A, H; Color photo on page 15

Moving Boxes

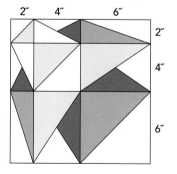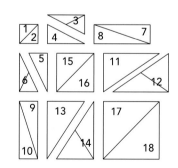

Patch	Cut	Subcut
1, 2	1 ea: 2⅞″ □	1 ea: ◺
3	1: A ▷	
4	1: A ▷	
5	1: A ◿	
6	1: A ◁	
7, 8	1 ea: B ▷	
9, 10	1 ea: B ◿	
11	1: H ◿	
12	1: H ◹	
13	1: H ▷	
14	1: H ▷	
15, 16	1 ea: 4⅞″ □	1 ea: ◺
17, 18	1 ea: 6⅞″ □	1 ea: ◺

Templates: A, B, H; Color photo on page 15

CHAPTER 4

Making AnglePlay Quilts

This chapter will open your eyes to many possibilities for including AnglePlay blocks in quilts. AnglePlay blocks may look traditional at first glance, but quilts that include them always beg for a second look! It's fun to make these quilts because the more the viewer looks at them, the more he or she discovers. In addition, AnglePlay triangles create the opportunity to play with optical illusions in pieced quilts by camouflaging where one block stops and its neighbor begins, as well as where the quilt stops and the border area begins.

Peruse the quilt photos and notice the role of striped fabrics, variegated fabrics, and gradations—fabrics that flow from light to dark (border of *City Lights*, page 52) or move from one color to another (border of *Desert Stars*, page 38). Some fabrics include a change in the scale of print (*Square Dance*, page 47) or are mottled in texture. Such fabrics create a more dynamic look to the quilt. Compare the line drawing of the quilt with the color photo and notice that fabric choices can create a very complex look in a quilt made from few shapes and simple piecing.

Please note that fabric requirements are approximate. I've tried to be generous, but striped and variegated fabrics are particularly hard to estimate; the number of repeats of the stripe determines how much fabric you actually need. Buy more of these types of fabrics than you think you'll need, or cut the quilt out *fast*, in case you need to go back to the quilt shop for more!

I encourage you to use more than one fabric for a given shape in a quilt. I've long maintained that it is an advantage to run out of a particular fabric in a quilt because it makes you go back to your fabric shelf (or back to the quilt shop!) to choose another fabric that sings the same song but provides a little more variety. Your quilt will not only be more interesting to look at; it will be more interesting to piece.

In addition to the color photo of each quilt, I've included a line drawing. Many of these quilts can be colored differently from the example in the photo to bring out other overall designs. Trace or photocopy the line drawing and play with colored pencils to see what new interpretations of these designs *you* come up with.

All the quilts in this chapter are made of 12″ finished blocks, unless otherwise noted. Review the cutting and piecing guidelines (pages 5–11) before cutting and sewing your quilt. Refer back to pages 6–8 as needed when cutting, especially for right-facing triangles (RFT), left-facing triangles (LFT), and Sections A and B. Guidelines for cutting traditional shapes such as squares, rectangles, half-square triangles, and quarter-square triangles are on page 6.

For pieced triangles (pages 7–8), Section A refers to the side triangle and Section B refers to the base triangle.

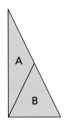

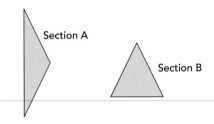

Cutting instructions are given for each fabric. A specific fabric may appear in several different blocks.

To keep yourself organized, and to speed the piecing process, make a paper "piecing tray" (page 9) for each different block in the quilt. As you cut the pieces that will make the block, put them in place on the appropriate paper piecing tray. Then you can use chain piecing to speed the block assembly process.

If you prefer to create your quilt on a design wall, place each shape in its respective place. When all the shapes are cut and it is time to sew, take all the similar blocks down and stack them on your piecing tray so you can chain piece them. Slide a small cutting board, hard ironing pad, or cookie sheet under the piecing tray to make it easier to carry from your worktable to the design wall, and vice versa.

NOTES ON QUILT BACKINGS

The yardage estimates for quilt backings are based on a length 8″ longer than the finished length of the quilt (the same size as the batting). For quilts wider than your fabric, you will need to piece the backing fabric horizontally or vertically. I often make pieced backings to help use up my fabric stash and make the back of the quilt more interesting. If the quilt top is wider than the backing fabric opened out to its full width, I slit the backing fabric along the fold. I then make a strip from the quilt leftovers (sew together simple strips or squares of leftover fabric) to insert between the two lengths of backing fabric.

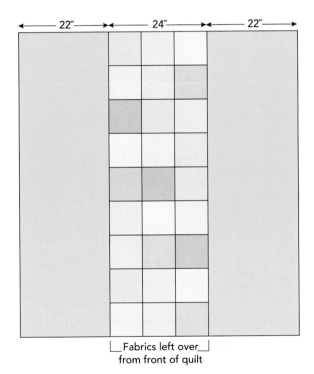

Making pieced backings

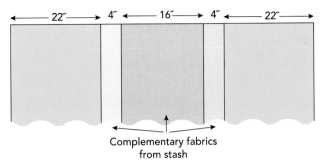

Making pieced backings

If the quilt requires two complete lengths of fabric, cut the backing fabric in half, slit one of the pieces along the fold, and sew narrow strips to either side of the wider one.

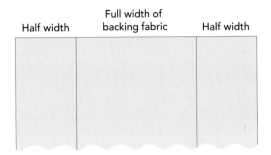

THE QUILTS

Each quilt project includes a special feature:

- **Summer Serenade** Sampler quilt, the AnglePlay way (page 30)

- **Midnight Sun Table Runner** Multiple versions of one block made by rotating block quadrants (page 35)

- **Desert Stars** Two different blocks that create a secondary design when set together (page 38)

- **Fourth of July** Blocks set together camouflaging where one block ends and its neighbor begins (page 42)

- **Square Dance** One-way (directional) designs (page 47)

- **City Lights** Multiple versions of a block made by dropping design lines (page 52)

Summer Serenade

by Margaret J. Miller, Bremerton, WA, 46″ × 60″, 2005.
Quilted by Kathy Sandbach, Bandon, OR.

Design Notes

In this fabulous sampler quilt, the blocks are in rows, but the sashing strips and border are pieced instead of being single strips of fabric. The fabrics and colors chosen, along with their placement, allow the blocks to "bleed" out into the sashing strips, camouflaging the boundaries of the blocks. You may substitute other 12″ blocks for the six blocks shown; follow the cutting instructions in the block pattern section if you do. To simplify the cutting instructions, the materials list calls for two lime green prints; feel free to use more than two, as I did.

MATERIALS

Templates: A, B, C, D

Rainbow stripe: 1½ yards for blocks, sashing and border units, and binding

5 Yellows ranging from light yellow (1) to gold (5): 1 fat quarter or ¼ yard of each for blocks, border units, border sashing, and corner units

Subtle green stripe: ½ yard for border units, border sashing, and corner units

2 Lime green prints: 1 fat quarter or ¼ yard of each for blocks and border sashing

Lime green: ¼ yard for border units

Dark medium-green stripe: 1 yard for border units, border sashing, and corner units

Bold green stripe: 1 yard for blocks, border units, and corner units

7 Pinks/purples in assorted prints: 1 fat quarter or ¼ yard of each for blocks, sashing, border units, and corner units

Backing: 3⅛ yards of one fabric (see page 29)

Batting: 54″ × 68″

BLOCKS USED

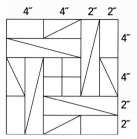

4″ 4″ 2″ 2″ · 4″ 4″ 2″ 2″

Block 1: Braided Bounds (page 22)

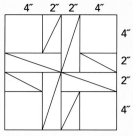

4″ 2″ 2″ 4″ · 4″ 2″ 2″ 4″

Block 2: Double Star (page 23)

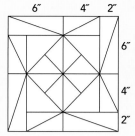

6″ 4″ 2″ · 6″ 4″ 2″

Block 3: Harlequin Var. (page 21)

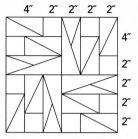

4″ 2″ 2″ 2″ 2″ · 4″ 2″ 2″ 2″ 2″

Block 4: Park Place (page 22)

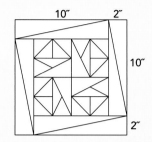

10″ 2″ · 10″ 2″

Block 5: Sparkle Plenty (page 24)

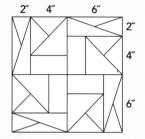

2″ 4″ 6″ · 2″ 4″ 6″

Block 6: Spinning Wheel (page 25)

UNITS USED

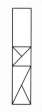

Border sashing
Make 6.

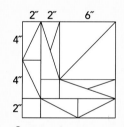

2″ 2″ 6″ · 4″ 4″ 2″

Corner unit
Make 4.

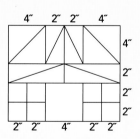

4″ 2″ 2″ 4″ · 4″ 2″ 2″ 2″ · 2″ 2″ 4″ 2″ 2″

Border side unit
Make 10.

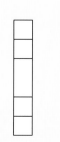

Inner sashing
Make 5.

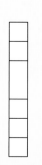

Center vertical sashing
Make 2.

Line drawing of quilt to color in your fabric choices

CUTTING INSTRUCTIONS

Pay special attention to the direction of the stripes. Sometimes the stripe is parallel to the long edge of the triangle, sometimes to the short edge, and sometimes to the diagonal.

Fabric	Block or Unit	# to Cut	Template or Size to Cut	Subcut
Rainbow stripe	1 Braided Bounds	4 LFT	A	
	2 Double Star	4 RFT	A	
		4 RFT	B	
	3 Harlequin	1	5 1/4"	4
	4 Park Place	4	2 1/2"	
		4 LFT Section B	B	
	5 Sparkle Plenty	2	2 7/8"	4
		4 LFT Section B	A	
	6 Spinning Wheel	2	5 1/4"	4
		4	2 1/2" × 4 1/2"	
	Border side units	10	4 1/2"	
	Border side units	10 RFT	A	
	Border side units	10 LFT	A	
	Inner sashing and center vertical sashing	7	2 1/2" × 4 1/2"	
Yellow 1 (lightest)	4 Park Place	4 LFT	B	
	5 Sparkle Plenty	2 LFT	A	
Yellow 2	2 Double Star	4 RFT	A	
	5 Sparkle Plenty	2 LFT	A	
	6 Spinning Wheel	4 RFT	B	
	Border side units	10 RFT	A	
Yellow 3	1 Braided Bounds	4 LFT	A	
	3 Harlequin	4 LFT	A	
	5 Sparkle Plenty	2	2 7/8"	4
	Border side units	10 LFT	B	
	Corner units	4 RFT Section A	B	
		4 LFT Section A	B	
	Border sashing	3	2 7/8"	6
Yellow 4	6 Spinning Wheel	2	4 7/8"	4
	Border sashing	6 RFT	A	
Yellow 5 (gold)	5 Sparkle Plenty	4 LFT	D	
	Corner units	4 RFT	B	
		4 LFT	B	
Subtle green stripe	Border side unit	10 RFT	B	
		10 LFT	B	
	Corner unit	4 RFT	A	
		4 LFT	A	
	Border sashing	6 RFT Section A	A	
Lime green prints	1 Braided Bounds	4 ea RFT	C	
	2 Double Star	4 RFT	B	
	3 Harlequin	4 RFT	B	
		1	5 1/4"	4
	4 Park Place	4	2 1/2"	
		4 RFT	A	
	Border sashing	2	3 1/4"	6

Fabric	Block or Unit	# to Cut	Template or Size to Cut	Subcut
Lime green	Border side units	10 LFT	A	
		10 RFT	B	
Dark medium-green stripe	3 Harlequin	2	4 7/8"	4
	Border side units	10	4 7/8"	20
	Corner units	4	6 7/8"	8
		4 RFT	A	
		4 LFT	A	
		8 RFT Section B	B	
	Border sashing	6	2 1/2" × 4 1/2"	
		2	3 1/4"	6
Bold green stripe	4 Park Place	8	A	
	5 Sparkle Plenty	2	2 7/8"	4
		4 LFT Section A	A	
	6 Spinning Wheel	4 RFT Section A	B	
		4 RFT Section B	B	
		2	5 1/4"	4
	Border side units	10	4 7/8"	20
	Corner units	4 RFT	A	
		4 LFT	A	
Assorted pinks and purples	1 Braided Bounds	4	2 1/2" × 4 1/2"	
		4	2 1/2"	
	2 Double Star	4	4 1/2"	
	3 Harlequin	4 RFT	B	
		4 LFT	A	
	4 Park Place	4 RFT	A	
		4 LFT Section A	B	
	5 Sparkle Plenty	2	2 7/8"	4
		4 LFT	D	
	Border side units	80	2 1/2"	
	Corner units	4 RFT	A	
		4 LFT	A	
		8	2 1/2"	
	Border sashing	6 RFT Section B	A	
	Inner sashing and center vertical sashing	30	2 1/2"	

RFT=right-facing triangle   **LFT**=left-facing triangle

BLOCK, BORDER UNIT, AND SASHING ASSEMBLY

1. Assemble the blocks as follows. Piecing trays (page 9) are helpful during construction.

Braided Bounds Variation
BLOCK 1: make 1

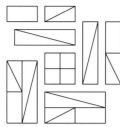

Braided Bounds Var. construction

Double Star
BLOCK 2: make 1

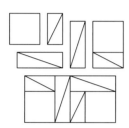

Double Star construction

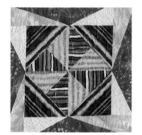

Harlequin Variation
BLOCK 3: make 1

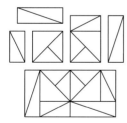

Harlequin Var. construction

Park Place
BLOCK 4: make 1

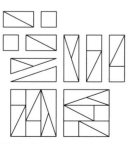

Park Place construction

Sparkle Plenty
BLOCK 5: make 1

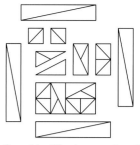

Sparkle Plenty construction

Spinning Wheel
BLOCK 6: make 1

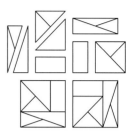

Spinning Wheel construction

2. Assemble the corner and border elements as follows. Scatter the pinks/purples in the border units so that you create Four-Patch units with contrasting values and prints. No fabric should touch another of the same value.

CORNER UNIT: make 4

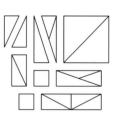

Corner unit construction

BORDER SIDE UNIT: make 10

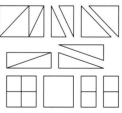

Border side unit construction

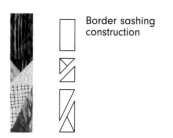

BORDER SASHING:
make 6

Border sashing construction

3. Assemble the inner sashing strips as follows.

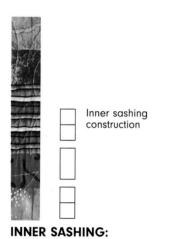

Inner sashing construction

INNER SASHING:
make 5

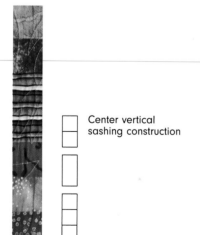

Center vertical sashing construction

CENTER VERTICAL SASHING:
make 2

QUILT CONSTRUCTION

1. Arrange the blocks, sashing, border, and corner units, referring to the quilt construction diagram. Be careful to orient each piece correctly.

2. Stitch the sashing strips to the block and border units.

3. Stitch the blocks and units into rows; then stitch the rows together.

Quilt construction

FINISHING THE QUILT

1. Since the design of this quilt camouflages where one block ends and its neighbor begins, it is fun to accentuate that effect with quilting. Let the quilting pattern "escape" the blocks and use curving lines as much as possible, since the sharp angles of the AnglePlay blocks seem to suggest curves rather than straight lines.

2. For an elegant finish, make and apply bias binding using the rainbow stripe fabric.

MIDNIGHT SUN *Table Runner*

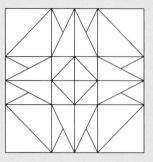

Unit   Rotation 1   Rotation 2

Design Notes

This striking table runner shows how repeating and rotating one simple 6″ square unit can make fabulous and intricate designs. Note how joining four of the units together in different rotations can create very different quilt blocks.

MATERIALS

Template: A

Dark blue: ½ yard for border setting triangles

Light to dark blue-green gradation: ⅜ yard for blocks

Light/medium blue: ¼ yard for blocks

Rust: ¼ yard for blocks

Orange stripe: ⅛ yard for blocks

Orange: ⅜ yard for blocks

Gold: fat quarter or ¼ yard for blocks

Medium yellow: fat quarter or ¼ yard for blocks

Light yellow: fat quarter or ¼ yard for blocks

Lime green gradation: ⅜ yard for blocks

2 Lime green prints: fat quarter or ¼ yard of each for blocks

Backing: 1¾ yards for continuous piece (see page 29)

Binding: ⅜ yard or use scraps

Batting: 25″ × 59″

Note: Use a very thin batting so candlesticks or vases won't wobble if placed on this table runner. There are also thermal battings that function as heat insulators, allowing hot dishes to be placed on the table runner.

by Margaret J. Miller, Bremerton, WA, 17″ × 51″, 2007. Quilted by Wanda Rains, Kingston, WA.

CUTTING INSTRUCTIONS

Fabric	Block or Unit	# to Cut	Template or dimensions	Subcut
Dark blue	Border triangles	4	9¾" □	16 ▽
Blue-green gradation	2, 4, 5, 6	10 RFT	A ◺	
		10 LFT	A ◿	
	4, 5	2 light	2⅞" □	4 ◿
	6	2 dark	2⅞" □	4 ◿
Light/medium blue	1, 3	6 RFT	A ◺	
		6 LFT	A ◿	
Rust	1, 3	6 RFT Section A	A ◺	
		6 LFT Section A	A ◿	
Orange stripe	1, 2, 3	4	2⅞" □	8 ◿
Orange	2, 4, 5, 6	10 RFT Section A	A ◺	
		10 LFT Section A	A ◿	
	4, 5, 6	4	2⅞" □	8 ◿
	5	1	4⅞" □	2 ◿
Gold	6	2	4⅞" □	4 ◿
		4 RFT Section B	A ◺	
		4 LFT Section B	A ◿	
Medium yellow	1, 2, 3, 4, 5	12 LFT Section B	A ◿	
	2	1	4⅞" □	2 ◿
Light yellow	1, 2, 3, 4, 5	12 RFT Section B	A ◺	
	3	2	4⅞" □	4 ◿
Lime green gradation	1, 2, 3, 4, 5, 6	8	4⅞" □	16 ◿
	1, 2, 3	4	2⅞" □	8 ◿
2 lime green prints	1, 4	1 ea	4⅞" □	2 ea ◿

RFT=right-facing triangle **LFT**=left-facing triangle

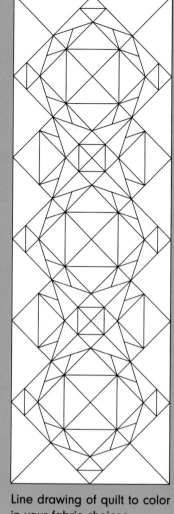

Line drawing of quilt to color in your fabric choices

BLOCK ASSEMBLY

Note that the 6″ block unit is a simple one, with only two pieced triangles in each unit. Make a total of 16 blocks with fabric variations as shown below. You may find piecing trays (page 9) helpful even for these simpler blocks.

BLOCK 1: make 2

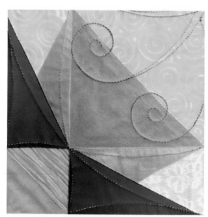

BLOCK 2: make 2

BLOCK 3: make 4

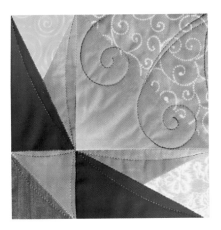

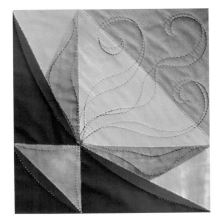

BLOCK 4: make 2   **BLOCK 5:** make 2   **BLOCK 6:** make 4

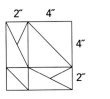

Block unit

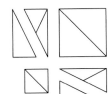

Block construction

QUILT CONSTRUCTION

1. Arrange the block units and setting triangles according to the block placement and table runner construction diagrams. Be careful to orient each block correctly.

2. Stitch the blocks and side (border) triangles into diagonal rows. Stitch the rows together.

FINISHING THE QUILT

1. Quilt your table runner, taking advantage of the "roundedness" of the 3 yellow/green areas; incorporate large gentle curves into your quilting design. Or, perhaps the points of the 2 inner blue-green star motifs could be accentuated by quilting star design lines beyond these shapes. It doesn't take very much quilting to make a table runner look good; after all, it is meant to be a base for candlesticks and centerpieces, not an art piece on a wall.

2. Make and apply binding using your chosen fabric, or piece scraps together as I did.

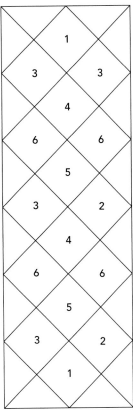

Block placement

Table runner construction

Desert Stars

by Margaret J. Miller, Bremerton, WA, 68″ × 85″, 2006.
Quilted by Wanda Rains, Kingston, WA.

Blocks and Units Used

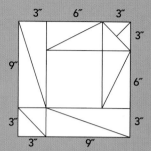

Baby Birds Var. (page 22)

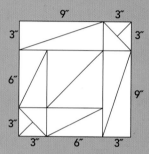

House Divided (variation of Masquerade, page 21)

Design Notes

This quilt is made from two very simple blocks; when set together they create stars that have both long and short points. You can make your own unique version of this quilt by rotating the blocks in place once you have them on your design wall. Note that the use of a subtle striped fabric in the outer setting triangles forms a simple but effective border for these stars.

MATERIALS

Templates: E, G

Medium-dark dotted stripe: 2¾ yards for border, blocks, and binding

Multicolor combed print: 1¼ yards for blocks

Red-orange to gold gradation: 1¼ yards for blocks

Loden green: 1¾ yards for blocks

Dark brown to rust gradation: 1¾ yards for blocks

Orange: ⅜ yard for blocks

Yellow: 1 yard for blocks

Light orange hand-dyed: 1 yard for blocks

Backing: 5¼ yards (see page 29)

Batting: 76″ × 93″

CUTTING INSTRUCTIONS

Note: The cutting instructions have been simplified to match the chosen block photographs. Feel free to vary the fabrics as desired, particularly for the quarter-square triangles that will create the pinwheels at the block intersections.

Fabric	Block or Unit	# to Cut	Template or Size to Cut	Subcut
Dotted stripe	Border triangles	18	12⅞" triangles*	
	4, 6, 7	3	4¼" □	12 ▽
Multicolor combed print	1, 2	14	6½" □	
		14 LFT	E ◺	
		14 RFT	E ◹	
	1, 2, 3, 5, 8	7	4¼" □	28 ▽ (need 26)
Red-orange/gold gradation	1, 2	7	3⅞" □	14 ◺
		14 RFT	G ◹	
		14 LFT	G ◺	
	3, 5, 7, 8	11	3⅞" □	22 ◺
Loden green	1, 2	7	3⅞" □	14 ◺
		14 RFT	G ◹	
		14 LFT	G ◺	
	3	3 LFT	E ◺	
		3 RFT	G ◹	
	3, 4, 5, 6, 7, 8	9	6⅞" □	18 ◺ (need 17)
	6, 8	6 LFT	G ◺	
		6 RFT	E ◹	
	7	3 RFT	G ◹	
		3 LFT	E ◺	
Dark brown/rust gradation	1, 2	7	3⅞" □	14 ◺
	3, 4, 5, 6	5	4¼" □	20 ▽
	3, 4, 5, 6 (dark along diagonal)	5	6⅞" □	10 ◺
	7, 8	4	6⅞" □	8 ◺ (need 7)
	3, 4, 5, 7	11 LFT	G ◺	
		11 RFT	E ◹	
	4, 5, 6, 8	11 RFT	G ◹	
		11 LFT	E ◺	
Orange	1, 2, 3, 4, 5, 6, 7, 8	10	4¼" □	40 ▽ (need 38)
Yellow	2, 3, 4, 7	17 LFT	E ◺	
		17 RFT	E ◹	
	5, 6, 8	7 LFT	G ◺	
		7 RFT	G ◹	
Light orange hand-dyed	1, 5, 6, 8	14 LFT	E ◺	
		14 RFT	E ◹	
	3, 4, 7	10 LFT	G ◺	
		10 RFT	G ◹	

RFT=right-facing triangle **LFT**=left-facing triangle
* See page 40 to make a template.

Cutting the Corner Unit

1. Draw a 12″ right triangle on graph paper. Cut on the drawn lines. Seam allowances will be added when cutting the fabric. Draw an arrow along the long edge to indicate the straight grain.

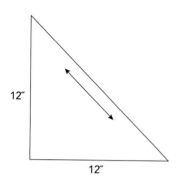

12″

12″

Corner and edge triangles; cut 18

2. Place the arrow edge on the straight grain of the fabric, so that the arrow is running the same direction as the stripe.

3. Stack several fabrics, adhere the paper pattern with removable adhesive (the kind used for scrapbooking), and cut out, adding a ¼″ seam allowance with a rotary ruler. The straight grain and the stripe will frame the quilt.

BLOCK ASSEMBLY

There are only two different blocks, but a piecing tray (page 9) will be helpful. Make the blocks using the photographs below as guidance for the fabric variations.

Block 1: make 7

Block 2: make 7

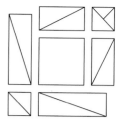
Baby Birds variation, Blocks 1 and 2 construction

Block 3: make 3

Block 4: make 4

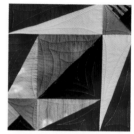
Block 5: make 1

Block 6: make 2

Block 7: make 3

Block 8: make 4

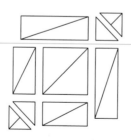
House Divided, Blocks 3, 4, 5, 6, 7, and 8 construction

QUILT CONSTRUCTION

1. Arrange the blocks by referring to the block placement and quilt construction diagrams. Be sure to orient each block correctly.

2. Stitch the blocks into diagonal rows, with border triangles on the ends of each row; then stitch the rows together.

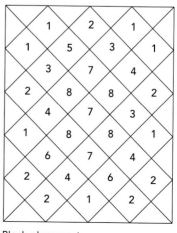

Block placement

Line drawing of quilt to color in your fabric choices

FINISHING THE QUILT

1. Quilt as desired.

2. Make and apply binding using your favorite method.

Quilt construction

Fourth of July

Design Notes
In this quilt, I've used AnglePlay blocks to create optical illusions. Though it looks like this is a 4-block quilt, there are actually 13 blocks on point in all, made from two different block patterns—Centrifugal Star (page 21) and Scout's Star (page 22). A couple of design lines in Centrifugal Star have been altered to create the dark blue angled border. Pieced setting triangles complete the framing of the quilt. Careful fabric placement and the use of variegated fabrics help to camouflage where one block ends and its neighbor begins.

by Margaret J. Miller, Bremerton, WA, 51″ × 51″, 2006. Quilted by Wanda Rains, Kingston, WA.

MATERIALS

Templates: E, G

Green to yellow polka dot: ⅝ yard for blocks

Red/gold stripe: ½ yard for blocks and border triangles

Light yellows (2 prints): ¼ yard of each for blocks

Gold: ⅜ yard for blocks

Purple to red polka dot: ¾ yard for blocks

Red/purple wavy stripe: ⅜ yard for blocks and border triangles

Red dot on ecru: ⅝ yard for blocks

Yellow zigzag: ⅜ yard for blocks

Purple stripe: 1 yard for border triangles, corners, and binding

Periwinkle: ⅝ yard for blocks and border triangles

Blue batik: ⅜ yard for blocks

Light blue: ¼ yard for blocks

Medium blue: ¼ yard for blocks

White: 4¼″ × 4¼″ square for center block

Dark blue: ¾ yard for blocks and border triangles

Backing: 3⅜ yards (see page 29)

Batting: 59″ × 59″

Removable adhesive (the kind used in scrapbooking)

Line drawing of quilt to color in your fabric choices

Blocks and Units Used

There are two different blocks, two border triangles, and a simple pieced corner triangle in this quilt, as shown below.

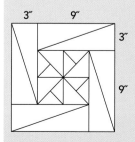

Centrifugal Star variation
(page 21)

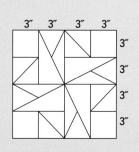

Scout's Star (page 22)

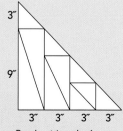

Border triangle 1

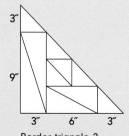

Border triangle 2

Corner triangle
unit

CUTTING INSTRUCTIONS

Review the guidelines in Making Pieced Triangles (pages 7–8) to cut the A and B sections. Some of the diagonals in the Centrifugal Star were changed in some blocks, and the center has different combinations of half-square and quarter-square triangles. Use Post-it notes on your colored-in line drawing to mask all but the block you are working on.

Note that the optical illusion of this quilt is strengthened by the use of variegated fabrics. Use the block photos on page 45 as a guide to cutting striped and variegated fabrics.

Fabric	Block or Unit	# to Cut	Template or Size to Cut	Subcut
Green to yellow polka dot	1	8	3½" □	
		8 LFT Section B	E ◁	
		4	3⅞" □	8 △
	3	2 LFT	G ◿	
		1	3⅞" □	2 △
	4, 5, 6	6 LFT	G ◿	
		3	3⅞" □	6 △
Red/gold stripe	1	4	3⅞" □	8 △
		8 LFT Section A	E ◁	
	Border triangle 1	4 LFT	E ◿	
	Border triangle 2	4 RFT	E ◺	
Light yellow 1	1, 2	8 LFT	E ◿	
Light yellow 2	1, 2	8 LFT	E ◿	
Gold	2	8 LFT Section A	E ◁	
		4	3⅞" □	8 △
Purple to red polka dot	2	8	3½" □	
		8 LFT Section B	E ◁	
		4	3⅞" □	8 △
	3	2 LFT	G ◿	
		1	3⅞" □	2 △
	4, 5, 7	6 LFT	G ◿	
		3	3⅞" □	6 △

Fabric	Block or Unit	# to Cut	Template or Size to Cut	Subcut
Red/purple wavy stripe	3, 4, 5, 7	8 LFT	G ◿	
	Border triangle 1, Border triangle 2	4	3⅞" □	8 △
Red dot on ecru	4, 5, 6, 7	16 LFT	G ◿	
Yellow zigzag	3, 4, 5, 6	8 LFT	G ◿	
Purple stripe	Corner triangles	8	6⅞" right triangle*	
	Border triangle 1	4 LFT	E ◿	
	Border triangle 1, Border triangle 2	4	3⅞" □	8 △
	Border triangle 2	4 RFT	E ◺	
Periwinkle	4, 5, 6, 7	12 RFT	G ◺	
	Border triangle 1, Border triangle 2	8 LFT	G ◿	
Blue batik	4, 5, 6, 7	16	3⅞" □	32 △
Light blue	4, 5, 6, 7	5	4¼" □	20 ▽
Medium blue	4, 5, 6, 7	5	4¼" □	20 ▽
White	3	1	4¼" □	4 ▽
Dark blue	3	1	4¼" □	4 ▽
	4, 5, 6, 7	12 RFT	G ◺	
	Border triangle 1, Border triangle 2	8 LFT	G ◿	
	Border triangle 1, Border triangle 2	8	4¼" □	32 ▽

RFT=right-facing triangle   **LFT**=left-facing triangle
* See page 46 to make a template.

BLOCK ASSEMBLY

Piecing trays (page 9) are helpful for the blocks. To create the 4-block illusion, make 13 blocks in the following fabric combinations. Note the slight variations in the Centrifugal Star block that create the dark angled borders within the quilt.

BLOCK 1: make 2

Block 2: make 2

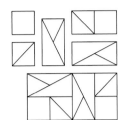

Scout's Star, Blocks 1 and 2 construction

BLOCK 3: make 1

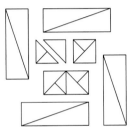

Centrifugal Star, Block 3 construction
Blocks 4, 5, 6, and 7 have similar construction.

BLOCK 4: make 2

BLOCK 5: make 2

BLOCK 6: make 2

BLOCK 7: make 2

BORDER TRIANGLE 1: make 4

BORDER TRIANGLE 2: make 4

CORNER UNIT ASSEMBLY

1. Draw the 6″ right triangle on graph paper. Cut on the drawn line. Seam allowances will be added later. The arrow on the triangle indicates the straight grain.

2. Place the arrow edge on the straight grain of the fabric, so that the arrow is running the same direction as the stripe.

3. Stack several layers of the fabric, if desired, making sure that the stripes are all running in the same direction. Adhere the paper pattern with removable adhesive and cut out, adding a ¼″ seam allowance with your rotary ruler. This way the outer edges of the quilt will be on the straight grain, and the stripe will frame the quilt.

4. Sew the triangles together in pairs to make 4 pieced corner units.

QUILT CONSTRUCTION

1. Arrange the blocks and border triangles as shown in the block placement diagram. Be careful to orient each block correctly.

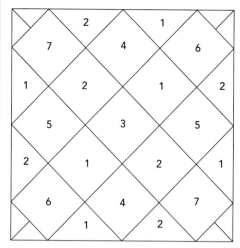

Block placement

2. Sew the blocks and border triangles into rows as shown; then sew the rows together.

FINISHING THE QUILT

1. Choose a quilting design that highlights the larger red and yellow pinwheels; this will further disguise the fact that this is a 13-block quilt, not a 4-block quilt.

2. Make and apply binding using your favorite method. If using a stripe, cut strips on the bias for added interest, as I did on my quilt.

Quilt construction

Square Dance

by Margaret J. Miller, Bremerton, WA, 68″ × 85″, 2007. Quilted by Wanda Rains, Kingston, WA.

Design Notes

This quilt is based on three block patterns and introduces the use of one-way designs and re-arranged blocks as a design element. The use of fabrics in color gradations makes the blocks in the center "glow." Note also the effective use of a multicolor stripe in the setting triangles, which creates a border around the quilt.

MATERIALS

Templates: A, B, C, E, G, H, J, K

Multicolor wavy stripe: 3 yards for setting triangles, blocks, and binding

Multicolor combed print: ¾ yard for blocks

Light to dark green gradation: 1½ yards for blocks

Yellow to orange gradation: ¼ yard for blocks

Yellow: 1½ yards for blocks

Pale lime green: ¼ yard for blocks

Light magenta: ½ yard for blocks

Dark magenta: 1¾ yards for blocks

Orange: 1½ yards for blocks

Rust: 1 yard for blocks

Backing: 5½ yards (see page 29)

Batting: 76″ × 93″

Removable adhesive (the kind used in scrapbooking)

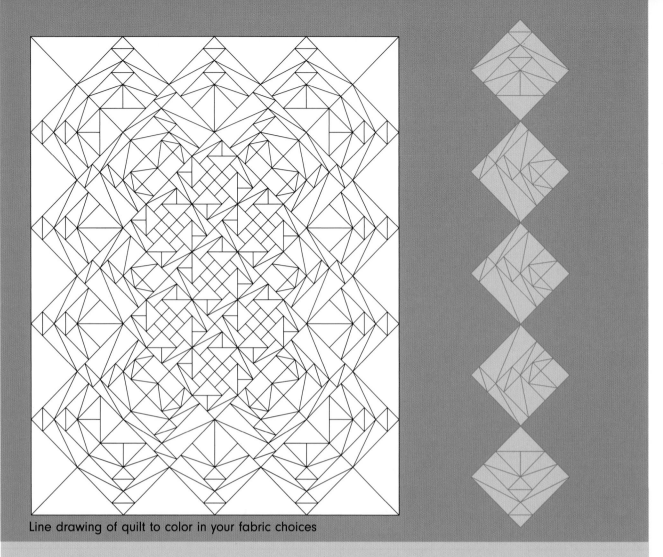

Line drawing of quilt to color in your fabric choices

Blocks Used **Note:** see page 50 for corresponding block numbers.

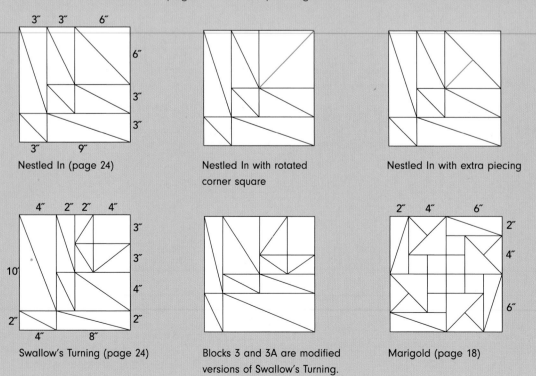

Nestled In (page 24)

Nestled In with rotated corner square

Nestled In with extra piecing

Swallow's Turning (page 24)

Blocks 3 and 3A are modified versions of Swallow's Turning.

Marigold (page 18)

CUTTING INSTRUCTIONS

Note: The cutting instructions have been simplified to match the chosen block photographs. Feel free to vary the fabrics and their placement as desired, particularly in blocks 5 and 6 where I've varied the placement of squares and quarter-square triangles.

Fabric	Block or Unit	# to Cut	Template or Size to Cut	Subcut
Multicolor wavy print	Border triangles	18	12⅞" right triangles*	
	2	4	6⅞" on bias**	8
	3, 3A	5 LFT	H	
		5 RFT	H1	
		5 RFT	B	
	4	5 LFT	B	
		5 LFT	H1	
		5 RFT	H	
Multicolor combed print	3A	4	3½" × 4½"	
	5, 6	12 RFT	B	
	5, 6, 7	7	5¼"	28
Light to dark green gradation	1, 2****	10	6⅞"	20
		14 LFT	E	
		14 RFT	E	
	5, 6, 7	21	2½" ***	
		4	5¼"	16 (14 needed)
Yellow to orange gradation	5, 6, 7	21	2½" ***	
Yellow	1, 2	14 RFT	G	
		14 LFT	G	
	3, 3A	5 LFT	H	
		5 LFT	H1	
		5 RFT	K1	
	4	5 RFT	H1	
		5 LFT	K1	
		5 RFT	H	
	5, 6, 7	14	4⅞"	28
Pale lime green	1, 2	7	3⅞"	14
	5, 6, 7	7	2½"	
Light magenta	1, 2	7	3⅞"	14
	3, 3A	5 LFT	H1	
		5 RFT	K1	
	5, 7	4 RFT	B	

RFT=right-facing triangle   **LFT**=left-facing triangle

* See page 51 to make a template.

** In order for the stripe to run parallel to the diagonal edge, you must cut this square on the bias. Or cut 8 right triangles using a template for a 6" right triangle. See page 51.

*** These will be the squares for the center of the Marigold block. I cut them from rust and two gradational fabrics—one was light to dark green and the other yellow to orange. I cut 2½" strips across the fabric and cut squares from the strips. This gave me a range of colors from the three fabrics.

Fabric	Block or Unit	# to Cut	Template or Size to Cut	Subcut
Dark magenta	1, 2	14 LFT	E	
		14 RFT	E	
		14 RFT	G	
		14 LFT	G	
		7	3⅞"	14
	3, 3A	5 RFT	A	
		5 RFT	B	
	3, 4	6	3½" × 4½"	
	4	5 RFT	H1	
		5 LFT	K1	
		5 LFT	A	
		5 LFT	B	
	5, 6, 7	12 RFT	B	
Orange	2	4	3⅞"	8
	3, 3A	5 LFT	C	
		5 LFT	A	
		5 RFT	A	
		5 RFT	H1	
		5 RFT	J	
	4	5 LFT	A	
		5 RFT	A	
		5 RFT	C	
		5 LFT	H1	
		5 LFT	J	
	5, 6, 7	28 RFT	B	
	5, 7	2	5¼"	8 (5 needed)
Rust	1	3	3⅞"	6
	3, 3A	5 LFT	C	
		5 RFT	J	
		5 LFT	A	
	4	5 RFT	A	
		5 RFT	C	
		5 LFT	J	
	5, 6	3	5¼"	12 (9 needed)
	6, 7	7	2½" ***	

****To do the optional piecing for Block 2, replace 4 of the 6⅞" squares with 2 squares 7¼"; cut them diagonally twice, and piece two triangles for patch 2.

BLOCK ASSEMBLY

Make the blocks as shown below. When arranging the squares in the center of the Marigold blocks, alternate both color and value as I did in my quilt to create interest. Note also that I added some extra piecing to the Nestled In blocks to take advantage of the gradation from light to dark in the fabric. Piecing trays (page 9) are helpful for the blocks.

Nestled In
BLOCK 1: make 6

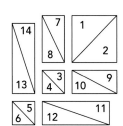

Nestled In, Block 1
construction

Nestled In
BLOCK 2: make 8

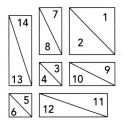

Nestled In, Block 2
construction

Swallow's Turning
BLOCK 3: make 1

Swallow's Turning
BLOCK 3A: make 4

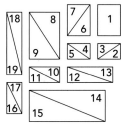

Swallow's Turning Blocks 3 and 3A construction

Swallow's Turning
BLOCK 4: make 5

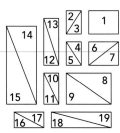

Swallow's Turning,
Block 4 construction

Marigold
BLOCK 5: make 3

Marigold
BLOCK 6: make 3

Marigold
BLOCK 7: make 1

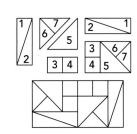

Marigold, Blocks 5, 6,
and 7 construction

CUTTING THE SIDE AND CORNER TRIANGLES

1. Draw a 12″ right triangle on graph paper. Cut on the drawn line. Seam allowances will be added later. The arrow indicates the straight grain.

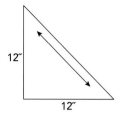

12″

12″

Corner and side triangles; cut 18

2. Place the arrow along the straight grain of the fabric, so that the arrow is running the same direction as the stripe.

3. Stack several fabrics, adhere the paper pattern with removable adhesive, and cut out, adding a ¼″ seam allowance with your rotary ruler. This way the edges of the quilt will be on the straight grain and the stripe will "frame" the quilt.

QUILT CONSTRUCTION

1. Arrange the blocks as shown in the block placement and quilt construction diagrams. Be careful to orient the blocks correctly.

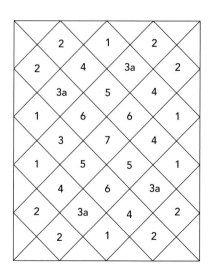

Block placement

2. Stitch the blocks in diagonal rows that begin and end with side triangles; then sew the rows together.

Quilt construction

FINISHING THE QUILT

1. Because of the angles in the blocks, this design lends itself to quilting that gives the impression of "scallops" around the edge. Quilt rounded shapes in the centers of the Marigold blocks to make the blocks seem more flower like.

2. Make and apply binding using your favorite method. I cut the striped fabric on the bias for added interest.

City Lights

by Margaret J. Miller, Bremerton, WA, 68″ × 68″, 2007. Quilted by Wanda Rains, Kingston, WA.

Block Used

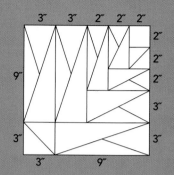

Half & Half (page 19)

Design Notes

This quilt is based on the block Half & Half (page 19), but it includes five variations of the original complex block. Each variation adds or subtracts one or more design lines from the original block. There are many ways to sprinkle color and value across this design. Put tracing paper over the line drawing on page 55 and see how many medallions and other forms you can discover with colored pencils!

MATERIALS

Templates: A, B, E, G

Green stripe: 2½ yards for setting triangles and binding

Magenta stripe: 1⅓ yards for blocks

Magenta bubble print: 1 yard for blocks

Brown to green variegated: ½ yard for blocks

Gold/brown splatter print: ⅓ yard for blocks

Orange speckled: ½ yard for blocks

Rust: fat quarter or ¼ yard for blocks

Blue, rust, and green print: fat quarter or ¼ yard for blocks

Dark leaf print: fat quarter or ¼ yard for blocks

Navy blue: ¾ yard for blocks

Green: fat quarter or ¼ yard for blocks

Orange to yellow gradation: ⅜ yard for blocks

Yellow to green gradation: ⅝ yard for blocks

Light magenta: ½ yard for blocks

Dark magenta: ½ yard for blocks

Red print, small scale: ⅛ yard for blocks

Yellow, orange, and blue batik: ⅓ yard for blocks

3 yellows, ranging from light (1) to dark (3): fat quarter or ¼ yard of each for blocks

5 orange to red oranges, ranging from light (1) to dark (5): fat quarter or ¼ yard of each for blocks

Backing: 4¼ yards (see page 29)

Batting: 76″ × 76″

12½″ square ruler

Removable adhesive (the kind used in scrapbooking)

CUTTING INSTRUCTIONS

Fabric	Block or Unit	# to Cut	Template or Size to Cut	Subcut
Green stripe	Setting triangles	16	12 7/8" right triangles*	
Magenta stripe	2	2	6 7/8" ▢	4 ◺
	3	4 LFT	A ◿	
		2	4 7/8" ▢	4 ◺
	4, 4A	8 LFT Section B	G ◺	
		8 RFT Section B	G ◹	
		16	8 7/8" right triangles*	
Magenta bubble print	2	2	6 7/8" ▢	4 ◺
		4 LFT	E ◿	
		4 LFT Section B	G ◺	
	3	4 RFT Section B	G ◹	
		4 RFT	G ◹	
		4 RFT	B ◹	
		2	4 7/8" ▢	4 ◺
	4, 4A	4	3 7/8" ▢	8 ◺
	5	4 RFT Section A	G ◹	
		4 LFT Section A	G ◺	
		2	3 7/8" ▢	4 ◺
Brown to green variegated	2	4 LFT	E ◿	
	3	4 RFT	G ◹	
		4 RFT	B ◹	
		4 LFT	A ◿	
Gold/brown splatter print	1	4 RFT Section A	G ◹	
	5	4 LFT	E ◿	
		4 RFT	G ◹	
		2	3 7/8" ▢	4 ◺
Orange speckled	2	4 RFT	G ◹	
	3	4 LFT	E ◿	
		2	3 7/8" ▢	4 ◺
	5	2	6 7/8" ▢	4 ◺
Rust	5	4 LFT	G ◺	
		4 RFT	G ◹	
Blue, rust, and green print	1	4 LFT Section B	G ◺	
		4 RFT Section B	G ◹	
		4 RFT Section A	G ◹	
		4 LFT Section A	E ◿	
	2	2	3 7/8" ▢	4 ◺
	3	2	3 7/8" ▢	4 ◺
Dark leaf print	2	4 RFT	G ◹	
	3	4 LFT	E ◿	
	5	2	6 7/8" ▢	4 ◺

Fabric	Block or Unit	# to Cut	Template or Size to Cut	Subcut
Navy blue	1	4 RFT	B ◹	
		4 LFT	A ◿	
		4 RFT	A ◹	
		4	2 1/2" ▢	
		2	2 7/8" ▢	4 ◺
	2	4 LFT Section B	G ◺	
	3	4 RFT Section B	G ◹	
	4, 4A	4	1 1/2" × 42" strips	8 strips, 1 1/2" × 18"
	5	4 RFT	G ◹	
		4 LFT	E ◿	
Green	1	1	4 1/4" ▢	4 ▽
	4, 4A	8 RFT Section A	G ◹	
	4A	4 LFT Section A	G ◺	
	5	4 LFT Section B	G ◺	
		4 RFT Section B	G ◹	
Orange to yellow gradation	2	4 LFT	G ◺	
	3	4 RFT	G ◹	
Yellow to green gradation	1	4 RFT	G ◹	
	4, 4A	8 LFT	G ◺	
		8 RFT	G ◹	
Light magenta	1	4 LFT Section B	E ◿	
		4 RFT Section B	G ◹	
	4, 4A	4	8" ▢	8 ◺
Dark magenta	2	4 LFT Section A	G ◺	
	3	4 RFT Section A	G ◹	
	4, 4A	4	2" × 42" strips	8 strips, 2" × 18"
Red print	2	2	3 7/8" ▢	4 ◺
Yellow, orange, and blue batik	2	4 LFT Section A	G ◺	
		4 LFT	G ◺	
	3	4 RFT Section A	G ◹	
		4 RFT	G ◹	
Yellow 1 (lightest)	1	4 RFT	A ◹	
	4A	2	3 7/8" ▢	4 ◺
Yellow 2	1	4 RFT	B ◹	
	4	2	3 7/8" ▢	4 ◺
		4 LFT Section A	G ◺	
Yellow 3 (darkest)	1	4 RFT	G ◹	
Orange 1 (lightest)	1	2	2 7/8" ▢	4 ◺
Orange 2	1	2	3 7/8" ▢	4 ◺
		4 LFT	A ◿	
Orange 3	1	4 LFT	E ◿	
Orange 4	1	1	4 1/4" ▢	4 ▽
		4 LFT	G ◺	
Orange 5 (darkest)	1	4 LFT Section A	G ◺	

RFT=right-facing triangle,   **LFT**=left-facing triangle
* See page 51 to make a 12" template and page 54 (step 4) to make an 8" template.

BLOCK ASSEMBLY

Make the blocks in the combinations shown.
Piecing trays (page 9) are helpful.

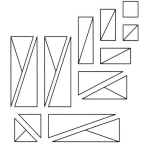

BLOCK 1: make 4   Block 1 construction

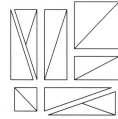

BLOCK 2: make 4   Block 2 construction

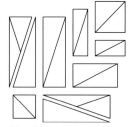

BLOCK 3: make 4   Block 3 construction

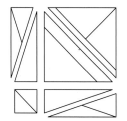

BLOCK 4: make 4   **BLOCK 4A:** make 4   Blocks 4 and 4A construction (refer to instructions beginning at right)

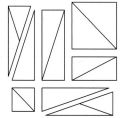

BLOCK 5: make 4   Block 5 construction

MAKING BLOCKS 4 AND 4A

To construct these blocks, you must first piece the square for the corner of the block.

1. Sew a dark magenta strip to the bias edge of a light magenta triangle (cut from the 8″ squares), leaving at least 2½″ of the strip beyond each of the triangle points. Press the seam and trim the strip, following the edge of the triangle.

2. Place a 12½″ square ruler on the assembled triangle so the right edges of the triangle are at the 9⅞″ mark. Cut the small points off the corners, as though you were cutting a square.

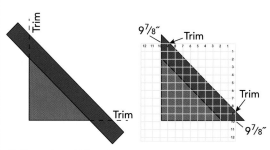

Cutting pieced triangle

3. Cut along the diagonal edge from corner to corner to make a 9⅞″ half-square triangle unit. Place on the design wall.

4. Make a paper template by drawing an 8″ square on graph paper. Draw a diagonal line from corner to corner in both directions. Cut out one of the quarter-square triangles for a pattern. Draw an arrow on the longest edge, to indicate the straight grain. Seam allowances will be added when cutting the fabric.

5. Place the triangle template on fabrics that have been layered right sides together, with the stripes matching. Using removable adhesive, adhere the paper template to the fabrics.

Place the arrow edge on the straight grain, and align it with the stripes. Using a rotary cutter and ruler, cut out the triangle, adding a ¼″ seam allowance on all sides. Cut a total of 16 triangles.

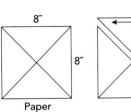 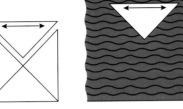 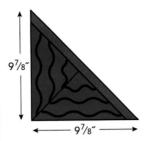

Paper

Make template to cut striped fabric.

6. Sew pairs of triangles together along one short side. Press. Make 8 pieced triangles.

7. Repeat Steps 1 through 3, sewing a navy strip to the diagonal edge of each pieced triangle from Step 6 and trimming to a $9\frac{7}{8}$″ half-square triangle unit.

8. Sew the units from Step 3 to the units just made to create the pieced square for Blocks 4 and 4A.

Line drawing of quilt to color in your fabric choices

QUILT CONSTRUCTION

1. After sewing all the blocks, place them back on the design wall with the green striped setting triangles. Try turning the blocks either one-quarter turn to the right or left, or upside down, and see what happens to the look of the quilt. You may discover a better arrangement for your blocks. Or, take the middle blocks and put them on the outside edge or in the corners. Be sure to keep your camera handy to photograph all the alternate quilt plans you like.

2. When you have settled on an arrangement that you like, sew the blocks into diagonal rows that begin and end with setting triangles. Sew the rows together.

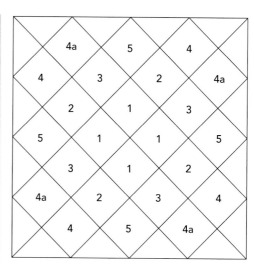

Quilt construction

FINISHING THE QUILT

1. Quilt as desired. Since this pieced design is so angular and pointy, soften it with as many curved quilting lines as you can.

2. For an elegant finish, make and apply binding made from the border triangle fabric.

Appendix A: Template Patterns

This section includes drawings of the AnglePlay™ template shapes used in this book. Trace these shapes onto heavy template plastic. Since you will be tracing around the templates onto fabric, a flimsy template plastic just won't do. Make your tracings carefully with a fine felt-tip pen and cut the templates out accurately with a rotary cutter.

On each template, the numbers near the base of the triangle are the finished size of the larger triangle; the upper numbers are the finished size of the half-size triangle. Don't forget to trace the half-diagonal lines!

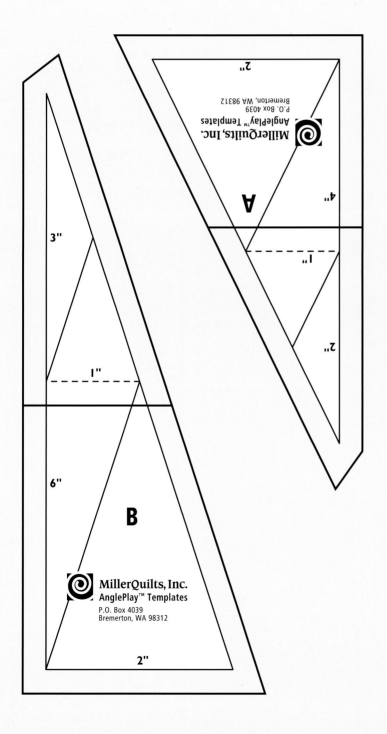

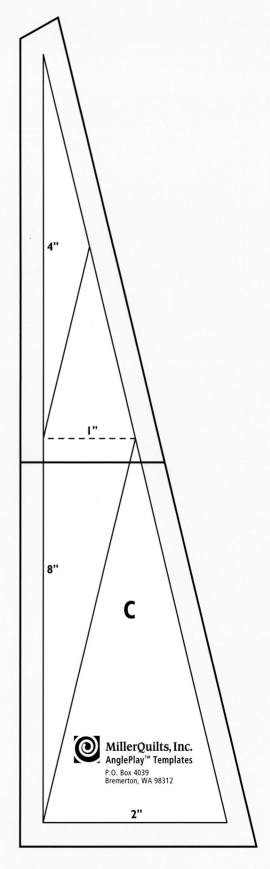

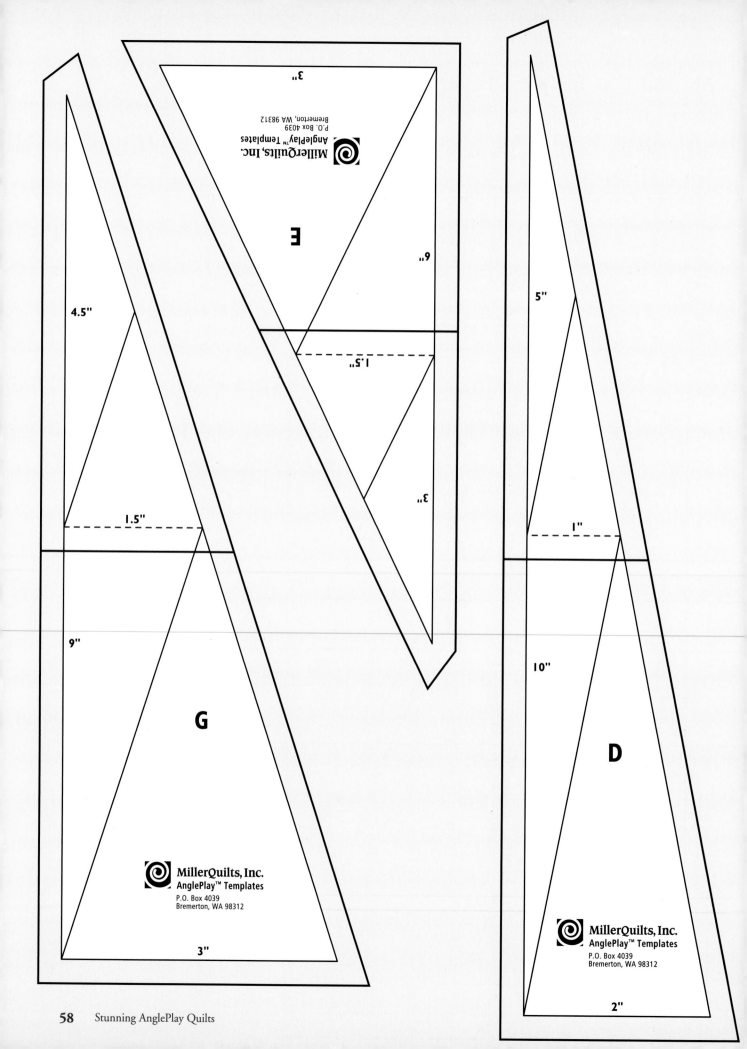

3"

MillerQuilts, Inc.
AnglePlay™ Templates
P.O. Box 4039
Bremerton, WA 98312

E

6"

1.5"

3"

4.5"

1.5"

9"

G

3"

5"

1"

10"

D

MillerQuilts, Inc.
AnglePlay™ Templates
P.O. Box 4039
Bremerton, WA 98312

2"

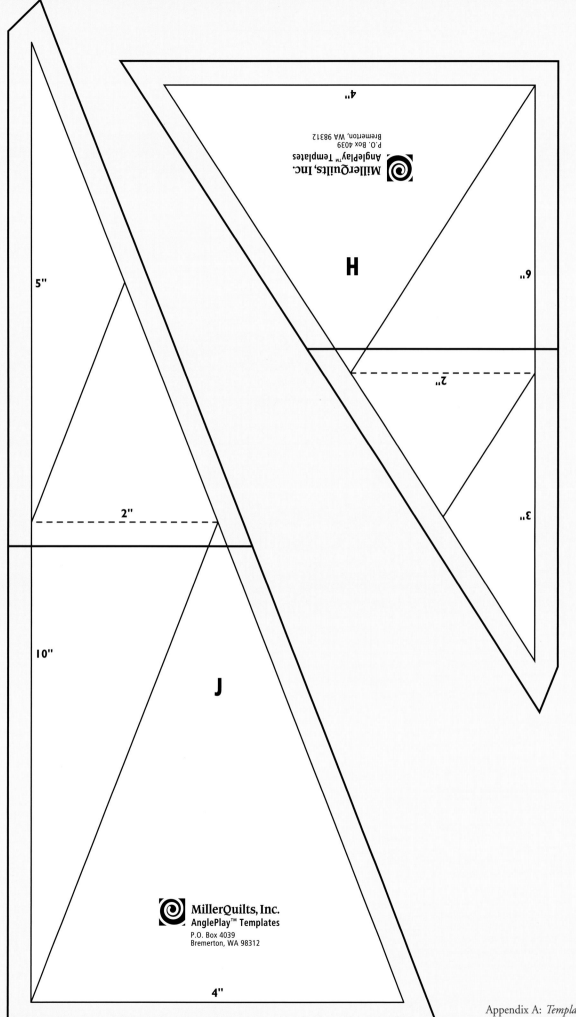

4"

MillerQuilts, Inc.
AnglePlay™ Templates
P.O. Box 4039
Bremerton, WA 98312

H

MillerQuilts, Inc.
AnglePlay™ Templates
P.O. Box 4039
Bremerton, WA 98312

4"

6"

2"

3"

5"

2"

10"

J

4"

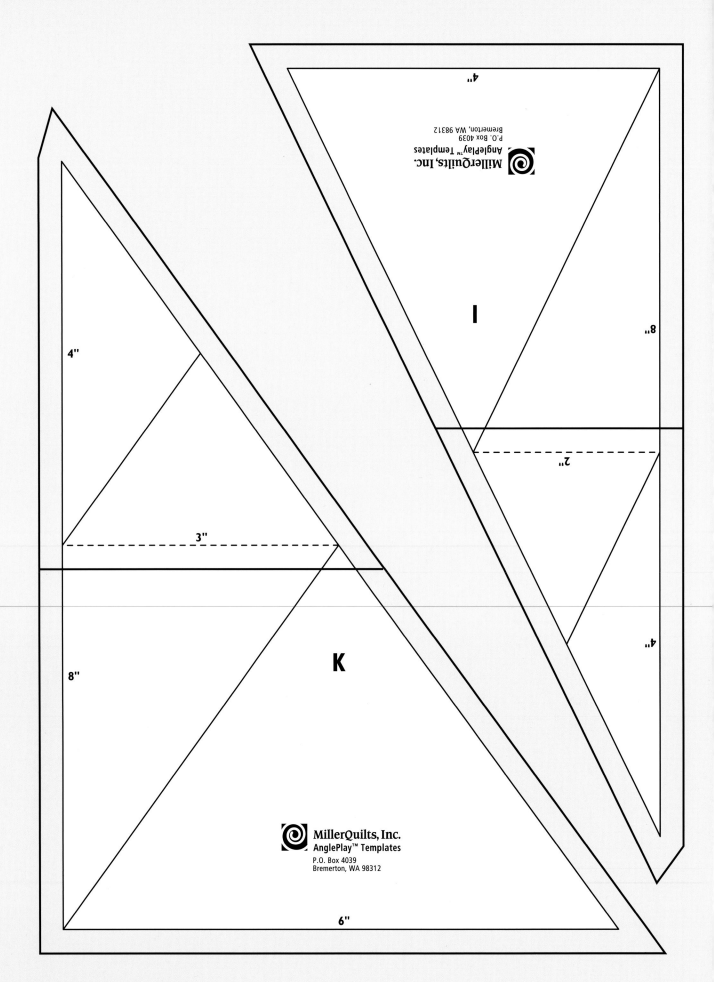

MillerQuilts, Inc.
AnglePlay™ Templates
P.O. Box 4039
Bremerton, WA 98312

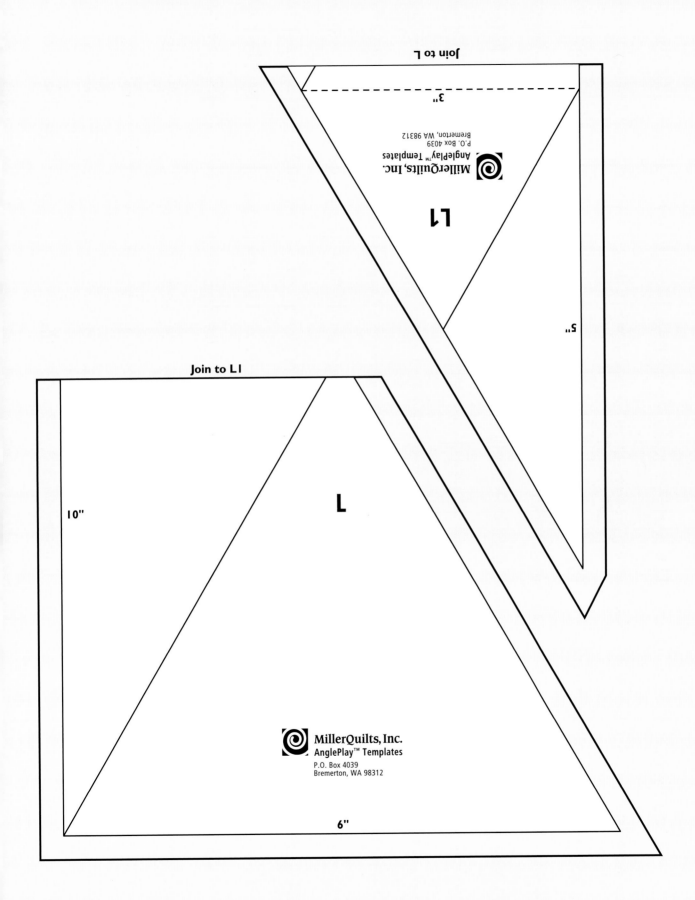

Join to L

Join to L1

MillerQuilts, Inc.
AnglePlay™ Templates
P.O. Box 4039
Bremerton, WA 98312

MillerQuilts, Inc.
AnglePlay™ Templates
P.O. Box 4039
Bremerton, WA 98312

L1

L

3"

5"

10"

6"

Appendix B: Block Index

Note: The first page reference is to the color photo of the block; the second page contains the shaded diagram with cutting and piecing instructions.

Resources

MillerQuilts, Inc.
P. O. Box 4039
Bremerton, WA 98312

(360) 698-2523
www.millerquilts.com

Your source for the AnglePlay™ templates, patterns, and books.

Electric Quilt Company
419 Gould Street, Suite 2
Bowling Green, OH 43402

(800) 356-4219
www.electricquilt.com

Almost all the AnglePlay™ block and quilt designs in this book were developed using the Electric Quilt 5 (EQ5) program.

The Warm Company
954 East Union Street
Seattle, WA 98122

(800) 234-WARM
(206) 320-9276
www.warmcompany.com

The color mock-ups of the blocks in this book were all fused using Steam-A-Seam 2, a double-stick fusible web produced by The Warm Company. This is a wonderful product for fusing fabric to fabric, or fabric to paper.

Wanda Rains
Rainy Day Quilts
22448 NE Jefferson Point Road
Kingston, WA 98346

(360) 297-5115
www.rainydayquilts.com

Wanda provides wonderful machine quilting services.

About the Author

Margaret J. Miller is a studio quiltmaker who travels widely, giving lectures and workshops on color and design that encourage students to reach for the unexpected in contemporary and traditional quiltmaking. Her full teaching schedule has taken her throughout the United States and to many foreign countries she would never have visited if it hadn't been for quiltmaking! She is known for her enthusiasm, humor, and sincere encouragement of quiltmakers at all levels of skill and experience.

The author of six books on various kinds of quilt designing, Margaret writes about quilting techniques that help students learn more about color and value almost in spite of themselves! Her ongoing passion is working with the long triangle, and she developed the AnglePlay™ templates so that the formerly difficult shape would be easier to work with. Explorations with the long triangle shape have opened up a whole new world of design to Margaret.

Margaret currently makes her home in her beloved Pacific Northwest, an hour's ferry ride west of Seattle on the Kitsap Peninsula. After 29 years of quiltmaking, her studio is finally out of her home, in a 900-square-foot building that was once a wood shop in the backyard. This building now houses the studio, office, shipping center, and warehouse. Walking through the garden from the house to the studio in the morning is a delight, especially when the birds are at the feeders and the flowers are in bloom. Views of the Olympic Mountains are never far away, just to keep everything in perspective.

Margaret Miller's Lectures, Workshops, and Products

For more information on lectures, workshops, and AnglePlay™ templates by Margaret J. Miller, write to her at P.O. Box 4039, Bremerton, WA 98312. Her current teaching schedule, lectures/workshops, and ordering information for her templates are available at www.millerquilts.com.

AnglePlay™ templates are indispensable for rotary cutting the half-rectangle shape. Each template has its elongated tip trimmed at just the right angle to ensure perfect piecing results, taking all the guesswork out of matching up two fabric triangles before sewing.

Miller, Margaret J. *EQ5 AnglePlay Blocks*, companion CD from Margaret J. Miller in association with C&T Publishing, Inc.

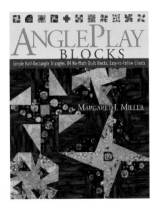

Great Titles from

C&T PUBLISHING

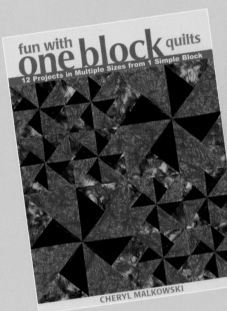